UPDATE AND HELPFUL TIPS FROM THE AUTHOR

Since my book was published in October 1987, I have conducted numerous aerobic walking clinics throughout the country. I will share with you some helpful information from those clinics. First, if you plateau at about a 13 minute-per-mile pace, you can increase your speed by concentrating on your arm swing which is about 30 percent of your propulsion. A vigorous arm swing in coordination with each leg swing is necessary to achieve top speed.

Second, the hip rotation described on page 82 helps lengthen your stride, but you can walk at your aerobic training range without it. In fact, you can walk aerobically by simply using correct posture and the bent-arm swing technique. If hip rotation doesn't come easily, don't bother with it. Third, the rhythm of your walk and your ability to maintain a fast pace is greatly enhanced if you use a Walkman with some up tempo music. Believe me, it really works!

A few more important tips are: Your walking goal should be to walk at least 3 miles per day, 4 or more days per week. If you are trying to lose weight, walk everyday if possible. The aerobic training range is now 65% to 85% of maximum heart rate and computation instructions are on page 55. Remember, your heart rate is always more important than your minutes-per-mile pace. Based on your fitness level, it will tell you if you are walking too slow or too fast.

Finally, proper shoes are extremely important to help you increase your walking pace and to enjoy your walk. When my book was published, an aerobic walking shoe was not available. Now, I can happily say that the *Aerobic Walker,* which I helped design for NaturalSport, is the first one on the market and it will help you walk farther and faster than you ever thought possible.

The *Aerobic Walker* will maximize your foot motion from heel plant to toe-off for a comfortable, sure-footed, aerobic walk. It has been tested by some of the top women walkers in America including the record holder for the 10K racewalk. They all agree it is the ultimate exercise walking shoe.

I hope you can come to one of the many aerobic walking clinics I will be doing for NaturalSport. If not, look for my exercise video on walking which will help you become a smooth, fast aerobic walker. Aerobic walking works wonders and it will change your life for the better. Go for it!

Happy walking,
Casey Meyers

AEROBIC WALKING

Virginia Sharp

AEROBIC

CASEY MEYERS

WALKING

THE BEST AND SAFEST WEIGHT LOSS AND CARDIOVASCULAR EXERCISE FOR EVERYONE OVERWEIGHT OR OUT OF SHAPE

VINTAGE BOOKS
A DIVISION OF RANDOM HOUSE
NEW YORK

A Vintage Original, October 1987
First Edition

 Published in the United States by Random House, Inc., New York, and simultaneously in Canada by Random House of Canada Limited, Toronto.

LIBRARY OF CONGRESS CATALOGING-IN-PUBLICATION DATA
Meyers, Casey.
Aerobic walking.
1. Aerobic exercises. 2. Walking. 3. Reducing exercises. 4. Cardiovascular system—Diseases—Prevention. 5. Respiratory organs—Diseases—Prevention. I. Title.
RA781.15.M48 1987 613.7'1 87-40076
ISBN 0-394-75440-9 (pbk.)

Grateful acknowledgment is made to Bantam Books, Inc., for permission to reprint two charts from Running Without Fear: How to Reduce the Risk of Heart Attack and Sudden Death During Aerobic Exercise *by Dr. Kenneth H. Cooper. Copyright © 1985 by Kenneth H. Cooper. Reprinted by permission of Bantam Books, Inc. All rights reserved.*

Design: Beth Tondreau Design

Manufactured in the United States of America

10 9 8 7 6 5 4

TO CAROL, A FUN-LOVING LITTLE GIRL,

A DEEPLY COMPASSIONATE WOMAN,

AN ELEGANT LADY, A WALKING COMPANION,

AND—BEST OF ALL—MY LOVING WIFE

ACKNOWLEDGMENTS

I could not have started with only the germ of an idea about our oldest form of locomotion, walking, and have ended up with a finished manuscript about it without the generosity of the many people who shared their personal knowledge, their private files, and their research material with me. I wish to thank each one and to acknowledge their contributions.

Early help came from Bob Gragg, a fifty-nine-year-old Centurion walker who led me to Larry Young, our only U.S. Olympic racewalking medalist. Through him I met Leonard Jansen at the U.S. Olympic Committee, who supplied me with invaluable walking research and technical advice. Jack Mortland, the publisher of the *Ohio Racewalker*, willingly shared his files with me.

Professor C. Richard Taylor of Harvard's Department of Comparative Zoology answered my phone calls and letters and made available important biped and quadruped locomotion research material. F. Clark Howell, professor of anthropology at the University of California at Berkeley, met with me and gave me many helpful leads.

Dr. Don Stallard and Loah Stallard supplied a wide range of medical publications. Dr. Gino Tutera provided an obstetrician/gynecologist's perspective on exercise for the women's chapter. When the manuscript was in its final draft, Virginia Frazier, a retired English teacher who is a local teaching legend, patiently combed the grammatical tangles out of it. Dr. Boyd Lyles and Dr. Arnie Jensen at the Cooper Clinic in Dallas, Texas, generously contributed their time and expertise to review the manuscript and to make constructive suggestions. Their encouragement for me to get the book published was 100 proof adrenaline.

And finally, I received most of the inspiration necessary to write this book during my daily walks in God's big outdoor cathedral. Thank you, God.

CONTENTS

PREFACE

Let's be honest about exercise. A vigorous daily exercise routine for most men and women is unpleasant to contemplate, difficult to implement, and even harder to sustain. We would all just as soon eat, drink, and be merry. When the excess pounds pile up, going on a diet seems to be a much simpler way to combat it than exercising. Dieting requires no physical effort, nor does it infringe on our time. The fact that dieting doesn't work for the long term does not seem to dissuade people from banging their heads against that same brick wall year after year. Chances are you have just finished a diet, are still on one, or are ready to go on one. Unfortunately, as medical evidence makes clear, the overweight problem can only be resolved by a combination of the right sustainable exercise and proper eating. In terms of weight control, the importance of exercise and proper eating end up in a photo finish. It is highly unlikely that anybody in today's sedentary environment will achieve long-lasting results without both.

To avoid exercise, most of us will gladly tinker with our eating habits and try every lamebrained diet that comes along. Therefore our major stumbling block to weight control and fitness is finding an effective exercise program that is safe, pleasurable, and easily sustainable. The best exercise turns out also to be the easiest: aerobic walking. In fact this book will show that for both men and women aerobic walking is superior to all other forms of exercise as an assist in weight control and the development of a high level of cardiovascular fitness.

The foregoing statement obviously invites a put-up-or-shut-up response, and that's what took me to the prestigious Cooper Clinic in Dallas, Texas, for a fitness test.

Dr. Kenneth Cooper, who really put the word *aerobic* into our language, is known and respected worldwide by the medical profession. Having sold over thirteen million books on aerobics and physical fitness in twenty-two countries, he is perhaps the single most widely quoted authority in the field. Professional athletes and celebrities (such notables as Roger Staubach,

Pat Boone, T. Boone Pickens) and people from all over the world come to the Cooper Clinic for physical examinations and fitness evaluation. Twenty-five major corporations send their top executives there for annual physicals. The clinic facilities are equipped with the latest state-of-the-art testing equipment. The outstanding medical and exercise staff reflect Dr. Cooper's thorough dedication to health and fitness. Over a sixteen-year period, Dr. Cooper and his staff have conducted more than 80,000 treadmill stress tests for cardiovascular fitness and endurance, accumulating the largest bank of experience of any single medical facility in the world.

That morning of June 3, 1985, as I got ready for my fitness test and the fifteen electrical leads were being attached to my chest, Dr. Boyd Lyles, the attending physician, smiled when he said, "If you're able to stay on more than twenty-seven and a half minutes, you will equal Dr. Cooper's personal best time. He runs three to four miles four or five days a week at a seven-minute-per-mile pace and is two years younger than you."

Twenty-eight minutes and thirty-two seconds later, I stepped off the treadmill exhausted, but more convinced than ever that aerobic walking is the superior exercise for everyone. Aerobic walking gave me the fitness endurance to beat not only Dr. Cooper's stress test time but also the times of a twenty-three-year-old professional soccer player and three NBA basketball players. In addition, on a chart called "Definition of Fitness Categories for Males" that was constructed from the extensive testing done at the Cooper Clinic, my time was one minute and thirty-two seconds better than the time needed for the top ("Superior") fitness rating of a male *thirty years of age or younger.* Not bad for a fifty-nine-year-old retired businessman living in a small rural county in northwest Missouri!

What is most encouraging about my test results is that I am not really an exercise bug. I have always viewed vigorous daily exercise as one of life's necessities I'd just as soon do without. I certainly don't want to do any more of it than absolutely necessary. For me, quail hunting and fishing are better ways to spend my spare time. I was fifty-two years old before I jogged my first mile. Three years later, I ended up with a knee about the size and consistency of an overripe honeydew melon. I did not like jogging. The nation was on a jogging craze, however, and like a lot of other unknowledgeable exercise sheep, I assumed the experts knew best and followed along. Now, after considerable research, I find that for most men and women jogging makes no sense at all. Fortunately, my forced search for an alternative exercise turned out to be an unexpected blessing. This time, instead of blindly following the advice of the exercise "experts," I began to question the validity of certain exercises as they apply to a person who is simply trying to maintain weight control and have a good level of physical fitness. Under close scrutiny, I found that many of the commonly recommended exercises were inappropriate and unsustainable.

If we were to approach exercise on a risk-reward

basis, evaluating the actual physical benefit we get for our investment of time and energy, we'd find that like a lot of other hastily recommended investments, often the reward isn't worth the risk or our time. Time is irreplaceable, and the older we get, the more important it becomes. You can't buy back last week or last month no matter how rich you are. Why waste time, sweat, and effort doing exercises that most of us don't want to do anyway unless we get maximum results for every minute we spend? Few people would invest money the way they blindly turn their bodies, time, and energy over to some young exercise jock in a fitness center. Even worse, the advice we get from some of the M.D.s, Ph.D.s, and celebrities who have written best-seller exercise books is either incredibly shallow or totally inaccurate. Furthermore, none seem to understand the true potential of an exercise as basic as walking.

As a regular reader of such business periodicals as *The Wall Street Journal*, *Forbes*, *Business Week*, and others, I have tried to write this book as one of their writers would approach a financial investment. In this case, instead of investing money, we are investing something irreplaceable and more valuable: our time and effort. To get the most from any exercise program, we should know the answers to the following questions before we work ourselves into a sweat:

- Which exercises help best with weight loss?
- Which ones are best suited for cardiovascular fitness?

- Which exercises have the highest risk of injury?
- Which ones are the most boring?
- Are all exercises aerobic?
- Which exercise gives the most benefit for the time spent?
- How long is it necessary to exercise? How often?
- When is the best time to exercise?
- Which exercises have the highest dropout rate?
- How effective is exercise equipment?
- What kind of shoes and clothes do we need?

You will be as surprised as I was when you find out the answers to these questions, for many of them will be different from what you currently believe. All exercises are not created equal. Some are clearly not worth your time and aggravation if you are simply trying to lose weight and get in good shape.

This book was specifically researched and written for men and women caught in the fat trap who are looking for a no-nonsense way out with the minimum amount of hassle. Studies show that the struggle with excess fat becomes relentless for most people over forty. But in today's sedentary environment even teenagers and those in their twenties and thirties are faced with weight problems. Although I have written this book from the perspective of a person over forty, I must emphasize that aerobic walking is effective for everyone regardless of age. In fact, the younger you start a lifetime aerobic walking program, the sooner you will be able to control your weight.

I do not represent myself as an "expert." Quite the

contrary; since I was not already ingrained with the existing exercise dogma, my mind was free to range farther afield searching for new interpretations or overlooked information. I found a considerable amount of both.

Throughout, I use the term *we* instead of *I* wherever possible, because we are in a fat struggle *together.* While I have been on both sides of the fat fence and am currently on the thin side, I view the problem in much the same way that reformed alcoholics view drinking. If they ever let their guard down, they're back where they started. Those of us who are overweight and out of shape have to stay on top of our fat problem the same way—one day at a time from now on.

If you are serious about long-term results, then you should approach exercise as a lifetime endeavor. That's why it must be injury free and sustainable. The scientific information and rationale in this book will give you the proper perspective on why you need exercise and why aerobic walking is the logical choice.

One final word of caution: Anybody over thirty-five probably should not engage in vigorous exercise without the concurrence of a doctor. And if your doctor smokes, get another opinion because he or she has more problems than you have. Doctors at least should know better.

AEROBIC WALKING

1. FROM CRO-MAGNON MAN TO THE OVERWEIGHT GENERATION

In many of the diet and exercise books that make the best-seller lists—books written by doctors, celebrities, quick-buck artists, or just plain folks like me—we are told we can eliminate the overweight, out-of-shape dilemma if we'll just follow their "newly discovered secret." By now we should all be suspicious of how many new diet and exercise "secrets" are left to be discovered. I have put my weight, physique, and energy level back to where it was when I was twenty. I did it with regular exercise and by altering the composition of my daily diet. Aerobic exercise and diet modification enabled me to drop forty-eight pounds and regain the energy level I had more than thirty years ago. You can achieve excellent lifelong results the same way. But there are no miracles or new discoveries. Every responsible authority I have read—and my own experience bears this out—agrees that permanent weight loss (generally accompanied by an increased energy level) can only be accomplished by a combination of proper exercise and proper diet.

The physiological system we have today is essentially unchanged from the one Cro-Magnon man and woman passed on to us forty thousand years ago. Anthropologists have established that the origin of man in various stages of development goes back millions of years. Present-day modern man, however, didn't appear on the evolutionary calendar until about forty thousand years ago. F. Clark Howell, professor of anthropology at the University of California at Berkeley and author of *Early Man,* writes: "At that point the people who made their appearance were virtually indistinguishable from those of today." *Homo sapiens* (modern man) had finally emerged from the long gestation of evolution.

About ten thousand years ago, human progress started its phenomenal escalation when man learned to grow crops and domesticate animals. Another major leap forward occurred about three hundred years ago with the start of the industrial age. In just this century alone, man has replaced the horse and buggy with the automobile, conquered the skies with the airplane, walked on the moon, and devised a weapon so powerful it could set evolution back a million years. As Professor Howell so appropriately observes, "The modern world does not stand still. What characterizes human culture is the increasingly rapid rate of its development. *It leaves biological man absolutely flat-footed, tied to the ponderous machinery of selection, which as we have seen, requires periods of time on the order of hundreds of thousands of years before it can produce significant differences in the human species* [my emphasis]."

There is an important link between today's population and the Cro-Magnon man and woman—biologically we are the same. This means our present physiological system is still programmed to function on a forty-thousand-year-old diet and a life-style that involved enormous amounts of physical activity. Modern technology, however, has changed our diets and drastically reduced our physical activity. In a study at Harvard's School of Public Health on the connection between exercise and fatness, the authors stated, "In his hundreds of thousands of years of evolution man did not have any opportunity for sedentary life except very recently. An inactive life for man is as recent (and as 'abnormal') a development as caging is for an animal. In this light, it is not surprising that some of the usual adjustment mechanisms would prove inadequate." Simply stated, the evolutionary process has developed our systems to function with considerably more physical activity than we are getting today. That's where the fat problem surfaces.

In the United States and other Western industrialized countries, an enormous number of men and women are overweight and out of shape. In *Scientific American Medicine* (1985), Dr. George F. Cahill writes, "By middle life, almost 50 percent of the men are overweight. Fifty to 60 percent of the women in the United States are significantly overweight by middle life. In men, the maximal increase in fat accumulation occurs in the third decade, whereas in women it happens in the fourth and fifth decades." Is that about when the pounds started to add up for you? Or was it sooner? Unfortunately, the conditions that brought us to our present overweight situation are deeply entrenched in our life-style and our daily diet. This makes losing twenty to thirty pounds or more and permanently keeping them off virtually impossible except by significant adjustments in our physical activity and eating habits.

Don't panic. We're not talking about acquiring the disciplines and sacrifices of a Carmelite nun. On the other hand, you need an immediate realization that this week's, this month's, or this year's newest ten-minute exercise or fad diet along with all the pills and potions pumped at us on TV and in magazines are pure hogwash. Our physiological system is still plugged in to the needs of our prehistoric Cro-Magnon ancestors. To fall for a "newly discovered" quick fix is just another exercise in self-deception. Unfortunately for some people, that's about all the exercise they get. I was in that camp for a long time.

It is important to understand how we actually get fat. In *Scientific American Medicine,* Dr. Cahill explains: "Fat accumulates whenever the intake of calories exceeds their expenditure. Fat may accumulate in an individual during periods of increased, average, *or even decreased caloric intake* if the person is not active enough to match expenditure with intake [my emphasis]." You need to clearly understand that last sentence. *Fat can even accumulate with "decreased caloric intake."* That's why trying to lose weight *permanently* by diet alone remains difficult at best. Exercise must become part of your life. I was fifty-two years old before that finally sank in.

Realistically, overweight people should aim to return to the weight and shape they had when they were at their leanest and fittest. Generally that was in their late teens or early twenties. For most of us, that is an attainable goal. Few of us can expect to achieve a weight and shape that are vastly different from the best we had in our prime.

We stop growing *up* rather early, but we never seem to quit growing *out.* Girls reach maximum height at about sixteen, while boys reach their maximum at eighteen, according to Dr. Anthony Harris in *Human Measurement.* Certainly, by age twenty-one, when girls and boys legally turn into men and women, all the expected vertical growth of the skeletal system is in place. Future growth, except bone density, occurs primarily in soft tissue. For most of us, other than athletes who purposely develop muscles, it comes in the form of unwanted fat. Excess calories inflate our fat cells with fat, causing stress on the joints and a drag on our energy level. For arthritics, unwanted pounds can make an already painful situation unbearable. It's important to remember, however, that being fat is no disgrace. Some people are born with a predisposition to fatness, just as some people are born with big noses, red hair, blue eyes, or any other physical characteristic over which they had no control.

Heredity plays a significant role in whether we are fat or thin. But none of us had any say in choosing our heredity. We were either lucky or unlucky. As Dr. Cahill writes, "Fat parents usually have fat children who usually become fat parents." How to break that tragic cycle is the subject of much study and little agreement in the medical profession. For those born fat, life is a relentless struggle between what nature dealt them and what our image-conscious society expects of them.

People who are fat now but had a fairly trim physique when they turned twenty-one can't as a general rule blame heredity. In most instances, the excess accumulation of fat that we often call middle-age spread is basically the result of caloric intake in excess of expenditure. The surplus fat was deposited in the billions of fat cells we all have. These cells carry the normal reservoir of fat we need to fuel our bodies on a daily basis. When we inflate those cells with additional fat, we're simply taking on more fuel than we're burning.

Among my sources of information, I found the college textbook *Exercise Physiology: Energy, Nutrition, and Human Performance* by William D. McArdle, Frank I. Katch, and Victor L. Katch to be invaluable. In a chapter dealing with fat cells, the authors state that, in round numbers, the average person has approximately 25 to 30 billion fat cells spread around over the entire body, while someone who is "extremely obese" may have as many as 260 billion.

Here's the kicker. Even if you lose the fat by whatever means, you never lose any of the fat cells. That means those billions of little fat cells are just waiting for you to go off your latest fad diet so they can fill up with fat again the minute your caloric intake exceeds your caloric expenditure. How many times has that already happened to you?

It is known that the number of fat cells becomes stable sometime before adulthood. Any weight gain thereafter is usually related to a change in the size of the individual cells, but according to McArdle, Katch, and Katch, *there is no biological reason for men and women to get fatter as they grow older.* Clinically speaking, there may be no biological reason for getting fatter, but from a practical standpoint it seems almost unavoidable. There are millions and millions of overweight people who are living testimony to that. To nail down *why*, we need to dig just a little deeper.

The fat equation consists of how many calories we take in and how many calories we burn. In order to lose a pound of fat, we must accumulate a 3,500-calorie shortfall from our normal ongoing needs. If your metabolism is such that 2,200 calories a day will maintain your weight without losing or gaining, then by combining calorie restriction and extra calorie expenditure, you can achieve a shortfall. For instance, if you cut back only 350 calories a day (which is not very difficult) and exercise enough to burn 350 extra calories (walk three miles, which also isn't difficult), you will have a 700-calorie shortfall for that day. Do that for five days in a row and there's your 3,500-calorie shortfall. You can kiss a pound of fat good-bye. Do it for a hundred days in a row and you can kiss twenty pounds good-bye. Too many people, however, skip the exercise and try to do it all by dieting. This gives rise to a constant proliferation of "new" and often bizarre diets of every kind imaginable. All of them are worthless long term, and many are actually harmful to your health. Some of the most unhealthy diets have been authored by doctors, believe it or not.

While dieting focuses only on caloric intake, in this book we are primarily concerned with *caloric expenditure*—or the lack thereof, which is a major reason most people become overweight and out of shape. To get from where you are to where you want to be will take determination, perseverance, and exercise—the right kind. Let's face it, there's a downside to the cars, golf carts, power mowers, automatic washers, and other energy-saving conveniences we all love. If we hope to stay in shape with today's sedentary life-style, exercise must become a permanent part of our life. But what exercise—and how much?

2.

POPULAR EXERCISES—PROS AND CONS

We all wish it were possible to achieve *Total Fitness in 30 Minutes a Week* (as the title of one popular book promised), but realistically, to achieve significant fitness and weight-loss results, it's going to take at least thirty minutes a *day*. Our sedentary life-style and overabundance of rich, fat-sweet food virtually dictates that exercise must become a lifetime commitment. There are few things any of us want to make a lifetime commitment to, especially exercise. Therefore, the exercise must be fairly natural to be something you'll do daily or a minimum of four times a week. To maintain that kind of regularity, it must be an activity that is relatively free from the risk of injury. It must be something that can be done anyplace, anytime, at home or away, to accommodate your schedule variations. For most people, expense is a consideration. It shouldn't cost an arm and a leg. It should also be an exercise that is nearly always enjoyable and at least is never dreaded. Few of us have the discipline to stay with an exercise we don't like.

It would be wise to choose an exercise that meets the 1990 objectives of the Public Health Service. That means it should be one that involves muscle groups in dynamic movement for periods of twenty minutes or longer, three or more days per week, and that is performed at an intensity requiring 60 percent or greater of an individual's cardiorespiratory capacity. This puts you into the lower range of what Dr. Ken Cooper calls "aerobic training." Dr. Cooper, who made the term *aerobic* part of our exercise language back in 1968 with his first book, *Aerobics*, says, "Aerobic exercises refers to those activities that require oxygen for prolonged periods and place such demands on the body that it is required to improve its capacity to handle oxygen." His research has shown that as a result of aerobic exercise there are beneficial changes that occur in the lungs, the heart, and the vascular system. According to Dr. Cooper, the common athletic activities that provide the best aerobic conditioning potential in descending order of exercise value are (1) cross-country skiing, (2) swimming, (3) jogging or running, (4) outdoor cycling, and (5) walking. I will show you how walking—if it's done aerobically—can move into a dead heat with cross-country skiing for number one.

Before we move to the basics of an aerobic walking program, let's take a look at some of the other commonly recommended aerobic activities so you can see why walking is far and away the best.

JOGGING

For three years, I jogged five miles a day, five days a week, at a nine-minute-mile pace. Basically, I always disliked it. I can't deny, however, that it helped me lose weight, raise my energy level, and feel better than I had in years—until my knees gave out. It wasn't until I began researching this book that I learned you have a one-in-three chance of injury from jogging each year, and a 10 percent chance that the injury will be serious enough to require a doctor. Those statistics are for runners and joggers of all ages. We can be certain that if statistics were available for only those of us over forty, the number of injuries per participant would be dramatically higher.

A fitness study conducted by the Canadian government showed that the dropout rates are higher for jogging and aerobic calisthenics than for any other types of exercise. The injury statistics of jogging tell why it is doomed as a long-term exercise. The Canadian study states, "One of the best predictors of dropping out of an exercise program is the occurrence of injuries." Most people, however, don't have any idea what kind of force their musculoskeletal system is subjected to every time they are airborne with each jogging or running step. According to exercise physiologists, gravity slams you back down to earth with an impact force of about three and a half times your body weight with each jogging step you take.

Dr. George Sheehan, medical editor of *The Runner* magazine, wrote a book entitled *Medical Advice for Runners,* which was largely devoted to injury. The final chapter in the book is "Living With Pain." That last chapter is about Dr. Sheehan's own experience with injury and pain from running and the emotional benefits he is able to extract from it. For most of us, however, pain is unthinkable as part of a daily exercise routine.

It is clearly apparent by now, the Achilles' heel (no pun intended—but it's a bull's-eye) of jogging is injury. The reasons for the frequency of injury from prolonged running and jogging are probably grounded somewhere back in our evolutionary past. As anthropologist Professor F. Clark Howell writes in his book *Early Man,* "Man is a creature whose evolutionary history has been one of adaptation to efficient upright striding and his way of life as a hunter-gatherer required a great deal of steady walking." Long before Cro-Magnon man, our musculoskeletal system evolved from a great deal of "steady walking." If you think about it, there was no other option. The hunter-gatherer only ran as his role alternated from the hunter sprinting in for the kill to the hunted running for his life from a man-killing carnivore. The musculoskeletal system passed on to us through evolution is suited for enormous amounts of upright, steady walking and only *infrequent periods of running* based on fight or flight. Running is a survival gait. The musculoskeletal system we got from Cro-Magnon man is essentially unchanged today. When subjected to the constant pounding of jogging, is it any wonder it breaks down so frequently?

We all readily understand breakdowns in mechanical equipment when it is misused. For instance, if a businessman bought a fleet of trucks with a half ton carrying capacity and loaded them with four tons, it would be no surprise if those trucks were plagued with broken axles, broken springs, and burned-out clutches. A woman who loads her electric blender with thicker, heavier contents than the motor can handle will soon have a burned-out motor. When we use mechanical things in ways for which they weren't designed, they will predictably break down. When we run for *prolonged periods*, we are using our musculoskeletal system in the same manner, and sure enough, it too breaks down. Prolonged running misuses our musculoskeletal system just as hauling four tons in a half-ton pickup misuses the truck. For some reason, we understand one but not the other.

For running and jogging to be so widely prescribed as a way to achieve physical fitness is to ignore its frequent harmful side effect—injury. Nobody wants a remedy that frequently is worse than the ailment. There has to be a better way for overweight and out-of-shape people to meet their exercise needs.

CROSS-COUNTRY SKIING

Cross-country skiing is most often cited as the best aerobic exercise of them all by exercise physiologists and is rated number one by Dr. Cooper. Cross-country skiers have to use a kick, stride, and glide action with their legs in coordination with an aggressive poling action of their arms. Cross-country skiing is a total upper- and lower-body workout utilizing all the major muscle groups. Aerobic capacity tests show that cross-country skiers are generally at the top of the list when compared with people who perform any other exercise activity. Cross-country skiing is relatively injury free. One ski is always on the ground, and there is no concussion on the joints. The muscles get all the action.

I got my first taste of cross-country skiing in the winter of 1985 on a trip to Vail, Colorado, and immediately became hooked. I intend to cross-country ski every chance I get, which might not be much, living in northwest Missouri. This probably answers the question of why cross-country skiing is not a suitable choice for your regular exercise. For about 90 percent of the people in the United States, cross-country skiing is nothing more than a theoretical exercise. No matter how good it is for you, how much cross-country skiing can you realistically hope to do? Someone seeking weight loss needs twelve months of regular exercise. Cross-country skiing is a superb exercise, but it is not available to enough people. Most of us will have to look beyond cross-country skiing for our main aerobic exercise.

SWIMMING

Aerobic swimming requires a pool long enough for swimming laps. There are few areas in the country where you can swim outside year-round. Only a small number of people have access to a large indoor pool. Swimming is primarily an upper-body sport in which the legs are used more to balance than propel the body. According to Jane Katz, author of *Swimming for Total Fitness*, in the freestyle or front crawl, the most popular swimming stroke, the arm pull provides as much as 80 percent of the forward motion. This means that unless swimmers also do accompanying kicking exercises they are not utilizing the major muscle groups in the legs enough. Because swimming eliminates weight-bearing stress on the joints, swimmers are spared the concussion injuries to joints and bones that joggers often encounter, but they have other problems. Many develop ear and eye infections, sinus problems, and shoulder injuries. Also, as we will see in a later chapter, most doctors recommend some form of weight-bearing exercise to help prevent osteoporosis. That means a woman who chooses swimming for weight control and fitness will also need a weight-bearing exercise to try to guard against osteoporosis. Aerobic walking is recommended for all three.

CYCLING

Outdoor cycling is frequently cited as another exercise that produces an aerobic exercise level if done properly. When put to the anyplace, anytime test, it falls short. For the most part it really should not even be considered on a risk-reward basis. Dr. Cooper's research shows that "a cycling speed slightly greater than fifteen miles per hour is the optimum rate for a good training effect." He says that speeds of less than ten miles per hour are worth very little from an aerobic standpoint. From a practical standpoint, where can most people ride a bicycle at a speed faster than fifteen miles per hour for twenty minutes without stopping? Certainly not in the cities. And a fall at fifteen miles per hour is sure to cause injury. For most people, cycling should be looked at as fun and recreation, but not as a main aerobic exercise.

CALISTHENICS AND AEROBIC DANCING

More than twenty million Americans are estimated to engage regularly in calisthenics and "aerobic dancing" (rhythmic calisthenics performed to music). The evidence is convincing that on a risk-reward basis aerobic dancing causes more body damage than it does good. In March of 1985, Scripps-Howard carried a story citing an article from *Medicine and Science in Sports and Exercise* that says *70 percent* of people enrolled in exercise-to-music classes *become injured.* Shin splints, stress fractures, and lower-back ailments lead the parade of injuries.

Lack of instructor certification is also a major concern when considering aerobic calisthenics. According to an October 1985 article in *The Physician and Sportsmedicine,* only "about 10 percent of the 100,000 instructors in the United States have formal training or certification." The certification process itself is unregulated and has no uniform minimal standards. Consequently, someone taking aerobic dance has no way of knowing if the instructor is qualified in the basic knowledge of either physiology or injury prevention.

Some people will put up with injury if they truly get aerobic results, but I don't happen to be one of them. Nevertheless, many determined runners and joggers keep fighting a series of continuing injuries because they are getting good cardiovascular results and weight control. In aerobic dance and calisthenics on a risk-reward basis, you get the *worst of both worlds,* in that you risk injury and achieve little. As Dr. Robert Kerlan, a founding member of the American Orthopedic Society for Sports Medicine and orthopedic consultant to the Los Angeles Rams, Los Angeles Lakers, Los Angeles Kings, and California Angels, says, "*Only rarely do we see someone who's achieved top physical shape strictly through taking an aerobics class* [my emphasis]."

RACQUET SPORTS

Tennis, badminton, squash, and racquetball are all great fun. Until my left Achilles tendon snapped in 1970 as I was going for a front court shot, I was a certified squash addict. Seven days a week wasn't too much for me. As aerobic exercise, however, racquet sports make it difficult to get the maximum effect, even if you play with great intensity. As Dr. Cooper points out, "There is a lot of stopping and starting, so the heart rate goes up and down and prevents you from getting the continuous aerobic effect that's available in a sport like jogging." If I had two healthy legs, I would still play squash and tennis, because they're fun. So should you, if you like any of the racquet sports. If you have a bulging waistline, however, you need a physical activity that will get your heart rate up into the training range of 70 to 85 percent and hold it there steady for at least twenty consecutive minutes. Racquet sports won't do it for you.

EXERCISE EQUIPMENT

When examined carefully for all of the criteria a life-time exercise should have, home exercise equipment leaves much to be desired. A lot of it is promoted by people more interested in profits than in health, who have rushed into the physical fitness boom to make a quick buck. All kinds of devices designed for you to push, pull, and pedal on are being marketed with slick ad campaigns promising aerobic benefits and better health. If a person is not careful, he or she will part with several hundred to several thousand dollars before realizing that many of these contraptions don't produce aerobic benefit—and they literally bore you out of your gourd. Most people end up quitting.

A *U.S.A. Today* story about home exercise equipment asked how long the motivation lasts after the novelty wears off, and a buyer for a major Chicago sporting goods chain conceded, "A lot of it has a life of about two weeks, and then it ends up under the bed."

One of the biggest names in the exercise equipment game is the Nautilus Sports/Medical Industries of Lake Helen, Florida. Their equipment is well made, top-quality merchandise featured in over four thousand health clubs and spas. But does it do what they claim? Their circuit weight-training program is advocated for developing strength *and aerobic fitness.* If you are a linebacker for the Chicago Bears or are in an apprenticeship to become the village blacksmith and need some bulging muscles, Nautilus will do the job. If you're trying to lose weight and develop aerobic fitness, save your money, time, and perspiration. In the April 1985 issue of *The Physician and Sportsmedicine* magazine, a study involving the cardiorespiratory effect of the Nautilus Express Circuit (NEC) was published. The study involved a twenty-minute workout on the equipment, consisting of fourteen exercises including five leg exercises, eight arm exercises, and one abdominal exercise. While it was possible to build up a high heart rate, the all-important oxygen utilization needed for cardiovascular fitness was lacking. The authors state, "Actual measurement of oxygen utilization indicated that the Nautilus Express Circuit does not stimulate metabolic responses to the extent implied by the higher heart rates. We concluded that the NEC elicits only marginal aerobic exercise intensity." What is even more important is that the fat-burning energy expenditure was lower than a simple, inexpensive exercise such as running (or—as I'll show you in the next chapter—walking).

Arthur Jones, the inventor of Nautilus, has been quoted as saying the Nautilus equipment is "just a more efficient barbell." Barbells are weight-lifting equipment used by muscle builders. They are not recognized as producing the aerobic benefit needed for weight loss and cardiovascular fitness. Don't waste your exercise time.

If Nautilus, one of the largest and most established names in the exercise equipment business, is throwing us a curveball by overstating what their equipment will do aerobically, what do you suppose some of the smaller companies are doing in their scramble to get a piece of the multibillion-dollar exercise market? On April 18, 1985, the *Wall Street Journal* turned a jaundiced eye on the home exercise equipment business and came up with a revealing story titled "ALLURE OF HOME EXERCISE DEVICES SPARKS BIG SALES—AND MANY INJURIES." One fitness expert told the *Journal*, "A lot of these things aren't made real well." As a case in point, the story tells of a San Antonio, Texas, woman who was impaled by the seat post on an exercise bike when the post sliced through the plastic seat. She got $900,000 in an out-of-court settlement. According to the *Journal*, the Consumer Products Safety Commission reported eighteen thousand home exercisers suffered injuries serious enough to require emergency room treatment in 1983.

Is all home exercise equipment worthless? No, but much of it is, for several reasons. First, it seems to require greater effort to get the major muscles in the upper and lower body to develop the oxygen utilization needed for maximum cardiovascular results. For businesspersons who travel and are away from home a considerable amount of time, the interruption of their exercise schedule eliminates their ability to obtain the cumulative training effect needed for fitness and weight loss. Another major consideration is that these unnatural, make-work activities soon become boring beyond belief.

Dr. Cooper, in his book *The Aerobics for Total Well-Being*, mentions exercise bikes such as the Schwinn Air-Dyne, where a pumping action of the arms is required along with leg movement, as giving aerobic benefit. But even with the equipment that actually produces a genuine aerobic workout, it takes a unique individual to be able to withstand the grinding boredom.

Another way in which someone can waste time and end up terribly frustrated when trying to find an exercise to help lose weight is to follow the advice of some of the celebrities who have written exercise books. Celebrity books generally are long on narcissism and short on well-researched information. *Jane Fonda's Workout Book*, with over two million copies in print, and her follow-up exercise tapes have been runaway best-sellers. She's probably made more money on the old discredited spot-reducing routine than anybody in the history of exercise. Fonda clearly says her various targeted workouts will reduce "fatty deposits." For example, in the section titled "Legs and Hips" she writes, "PURPOSE: To burn off the fatty deposits, tone, and strengthen the muscles. . . ." Her routine consists primarily of leg lifts, stretches, and flexes, and they will *not* burn off fatty deposits.

The real guts of Jane Fonda's fitness success is probably contained in two small sentences in her book. She writes, "I love running now. I try to do six or seven miles several times a week and three or four miles on off-days." *Now* she's talking about some serious fat-burning! Fonda is telling us she runs *a minimum of thirty miles a week*! Any woman (or man) who will consistently run a minimum of thirty miles a week and eat a low-fat, high–complex carbohydrate diet (as Fonda also recommends) is going to be lean, tight, and aerobically fit. On the other hand, if you have a weight problem and do all the exercises shown in the book but *don't* run or do some other extensive aerobic exercise, you'll still have a weight problem. Even someone as strong willed as Jane Fonda can't change that.

Another high-profile celebrity exercise author is Richard Simmons. He not only made the best-seller list by selling over half a million hardcover copies of *The Never-Say-Diet Book*, he turned the whole thing into a television show. Simmons has also warmed up the tired old spot-reducing routine and made a handsome career out of it. In the process, he has totally misled many people by denying the need for *aerobic* exercise.

The exercises that Simmons recommends—which are supposed to be superior to walking, running, and jogging—consist of "deep breathing, side bends, back and vertebrae stretches, deep knee bends, arm circles, touch your toes, mini sit-ups, mini push-ups, and *tootsie rolls*." Simmons's "tootsie roll" is nothing more than sitting on the floor with your legs out straight and rolling back and forth from one cheek of your buns to the other.

The exercises recommended by Jane Fonda and Richard Simmons as a way to spot-reduce fatty deposits have been totally discredited for some time by research from our universities and medical schools. In an article in *The Physician and Sportsmedicine* in November 1985, Dr. Bryant Stamford, director of the Exercise Physiology Laboratory and professor of allied health, School of Medicine, University of Louisville, Kentucky, wrote: "Performing twists and bends to melt off fat from the waistline or leg kicks to reduce the thighs has lost out to aerobic activities like walking and jogging; aerobic activities use a larger number of calories per minute." Dr. Stamford leaves no room for doubt about how fat is lost when he says, "*It is now well established that increased caloric expenditure is the only way to reduce fat—and that fat will be uniformly lost from the body, including the thighs and waistline* [my emphasis]."

James S. Skinner, Ph.D., professor of physical education and director of the Exercise and Sport Research Institute at Arizona State University in Tempe, was interviewed for an article titled "Of Magic, Miracles, and Exercise Myths" in the May 1985 issue of *The Physician and Sportsmedicine.* In the article, Dr. Skinner emphatically states, "It's been shown time and time again that there's no such thing as spot-reducing."

There are two things everyone should try to avoid when it comes to exercise. They are: wasting your time and going through unnecessary pain and discomfort. *Jane Fonda's Workout Book* manages to give you a big dose of *both.* Drs. Stamford and Skinner have explained that attempting to remove fatty deposits by spot-reducing is an absolute waste of time. In exhorting readers to "go for the burn," Fonda is also recommending needless pain. When it comes to exercise pain, Dr. Skinner labels the old "no pain, no gain" axiom as a myth. He warns that "it dooms to failure the kind of person who should be exercising. Pain is a warning that the body has been overstimulated. When you start getting that feeling, you should ease off. If you keep going until you get a burning sensation, you'll be more susceptible to injury and soreness. Pain isn't necessary to improve fitness. In fact, if you go for the burn, you're just going to slow yourself down for a few days. The body has its own wisdom." The next time some celebrity writes an exercise or diet book, approach it with caution.

It can't be stressed often enough that *the total involvement of the major muscle groups of the upper and lower body in a sustainable rhythmic action* is the best way to develop cardiovascular fitness and burn calories to lose fat. *When analyzed in total, the one exercise that tops cross-country skiing and all other exercises and exercise equipment as a way to develop maximum cardiovascular fitness and lose weight is aerobic walking.* It has no drawbacks. It passes *all* the tests. It is injury free, available anyplace, anytime, every day, at home or away, and it costs you nothing. Walking was fundamental in the evolution of the human species and is backed by over four million years of constant use from the early biped *Australopithecus afarensis* to *Homo sapiens* (modern man) Cro-Magnon. It has stood the test of time.

Some so-called experts have labeled walking a "light exercise." They have recommended it as a starter exercise with jogging or running as the ultimate goal. This is the conventional thinking, but it is wrong. The fact is you *never* need to run to achieve maximum aerobic fitness. All you have to do is walk faster. When walking is elevated to the aerobic pace, it can produce a superior fitness level. Walking is the one normal activity that we will all do at some level every day for the rest of our lives. Like many things in life, however, the obvious is often overlooked. Many people will be surprised to find there is more to walking than meets the eye.

3. HUMAN LOCOMOTION: HOW WE WALK AND WHY WE RUN

You are on your way to an appointment and you are walking faster than normal. Glancing at your watch, you realize that at this pace you're going to be late. You walk a little faster, but after a few feet, you suddenly break into a run. What made you do that? If you think about it, it wasn't a conscious decision; it happened as a natural reflex. At this pace you aren't running much faster than the last few steps you walked, but the run seems more natural, more comfortable, and easier than if you had accelerated your walk. You are right. You have just shifted your locomotion system into high gear and are cruising in nature's most efficient fast gait, running. *You are now starting to burn fewer calories and use less energy than if you had increased your walking speed to the pace you are now running.* This is probably the least understood of all exercise information.

We think that if we go faster—by running—we use more energy. But speed is not the determinant of how much energy we use; that is determined by the efficiency of the gait, not only in humans but in all animal species. A complete understanding of why aerobic walking (speeds of 12-minute miles or faster) uses more energy and burns more calories than running becomes important to anyone looking for the right exercise. There is more confusion and misinformation on this point than about anything else involved with exercise.

How we walk and why we run is what took me up the Old Causeway Road in Bedford, Massachusetts, one morning in July 1985 to visit Professor C. Richard Taylor of the Museum of Comparative Zoology at Harvard University. It is here that Professor Taylor and his colleagues have performed studies of locomotion on more than eighty species of animals—bipeds and quadrupeds.

A story in the December 14, 1981, issue of *Newsweek* magazine triggered my curiosity about Professor Taylor's work. The story told of Taylor and his American and European colleagues and their extensive research into how and why animals walk, trot, and run. What makes them change gaits? What gaits use the most energy? The studies revealed that the locomotion of all vertebrates can be described as the movement of either a spring or a pendulum. An obvious example of the spring is a kangaroo. Its huge legs propel it forward, and as they hit the ground, they are cocked to spring forward on the next hop. Their power comes from the elastic energy of muscles and tendons that is stored from the impact of landing. Joggers' and runners' legs work the same way, converting the shock of thumping down on the ground into an upward push. Professor Taylor estimates that "between 20 and 70 percent of the energy is stored and then recovered for the next step." As *Newsweek* reported: "That efficiency is actually bad news for weight watchers. Because muscles and tendons are so elastic, movement doesn't require much work and going faster doesn't necessarily burn more calories in covering the same distance. The experiments showed that no animal—man or beast—uses as much energy to move fast as scientists once thought."

Professor Taylor was extremely helpful in supplying me with biped and quadruped locomotion research for this book. He referred me also to the studies of Professor Giovanni Cavagna of the University of Milan in Italy, who with his colleague and mentor Rudolfo Margaria has worked extensively on energetics and mechanics of walking and racewalking in humans.

As their research reveals, man's fastest gait, running, is his most efficient and uses the elastic energy of tendons and muscles in a springlike action. It also uses less energy and thus burns fewer calories. The spring and the pendulum help explain an old biological mystery: *why animals, including humans, change gaits.* Walking is a pendulumlike movement and is entirely mechanical in nature. When people walk, energy from one step helps power the next. Just as pendulums have natural frequencies, so do pedestrians. When we try to walk more slowly than our natural pace, we don't make full use of our momentum. Conversely, if we walk too quickly, one foot has so much momentum that it starts rising before the other has touched down. Muscles, therefore, must work to keep it on the ground. Neither extreme is efficient, but fast walking beyond our "normal gait" demands more work and energy and burns more calories.

At the most extreme range physically possible, walking burns an enormous amount of energy. Olympic racewalkers achieve speeds of 6½-minute miles. In *Newsweek*, Professor Taylor said, "Olympic racewalkers are trying to lift the body and accelerate at the same time. Those guys are using two to three times as much energy to move as they would if they were running at the same speed."

Taylor's comment is borne out by a 1979 study from the Department of Applied Physiology at Columbia University. In his excellent book, *Racewalk to Fitness*, Howard Jacobson quoted the Columbia study by Professor Bernard Gutin and his assistants Jeff Young and Dan Alejandro. It found that at 5 miles per hour (12-minute miles), the runner burns 480 calories and the walker 530. The faster the pace from that point on, the calories burned increase significantly in favor of the walker. At 6 miles per hour, 660 calories are burned for the runner to 734 for the walker. At 7 miles per hour, the walker beats the runner by *270 calories*—960 to 690. Note also that the walker is burning *more* calories at 6 miles per hour than the runner is at 7.

The energy consumption of the walker was further confirmed in the college textbook *Exercise Physiology*, by McArdle, Katch, and Katch. In a chapter titled "Energy Expenditure During Walking, Jogging, Running, and Swimming," the authors write, "The mechanical efficiency of walking faster than 8 km per hour [12-minute miles] was one-half of that for running at similar speeds." They show a chart of oxygen consumption by walkers and runners as they increase their speed (see page 34).

The chart clearly shows that at 8 kilometers per hour, the lines cross. And as the athletes increase their speed, the walker uses more oxygen than the runner. To do this, the walker uses more energy and burns more calories. As you can see, the walker's oxygen consumption line goes up sharply after it crosses 8 kilometers per hour (12-minute miles) while the runner's line proceeds on a gradual slope. A good comparison of energy use can be drawn by comparing walking and running 12-minute miles or faster with two five-speed sports cars traveling side by side at 70 miles per hour. If one car is in the high-speed fifth gear and the other car is only in third, the car in third gear will burn considerably more fuel per mile. Also, its engine will have to work harder (run at higher revolutions per minute) to reach 70 miles per hour. Humans have only two gaits (or "gears")—walking and running. In the summary for this chapter, the authors conclude, "It is more economical from an energy standpoint, to jog-run rather than to walk at speeds greater than 8 km per hour."

This raises an all-important question. Who wants an "economical" gait if the main purpose of exercise is to

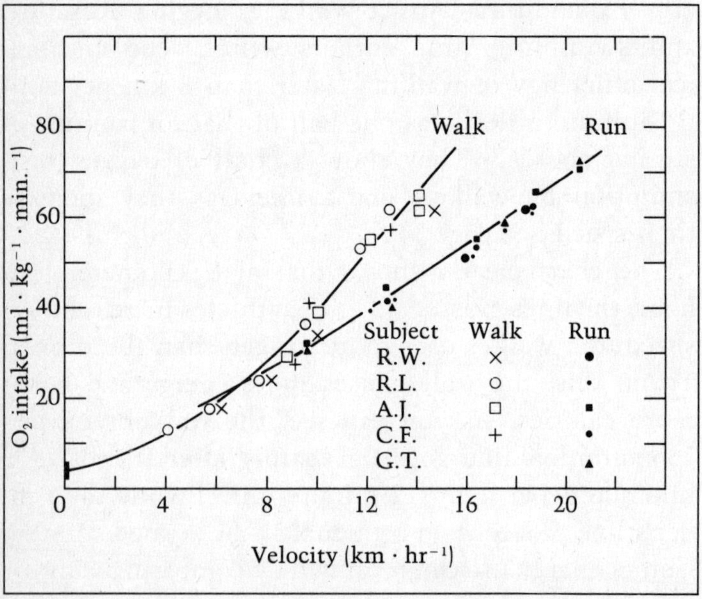

Relationship between oxygen consumption and velocity for walking and running on a treadmill in competition walkers. (From D.R. Menier and L.G.C.E. Pugh: "The relation of oxygen intake and velocity of walking and running in competition walkers." Journal of Physiology, *197: 717, 1968.)*

utilize major muscle groups to use energy and burn calories? After all, isn't that what you are trying to accomplish with a rowing machine, cycling, swimming, cross-country skiing, or any other aerobic exercise?

The walking speeds mentioned by Professor Gutin and the 8 kilometers per hour in the textbook chart are well above the normal range. In the next chapter you will learn that with a few simple biomechanical changes in your walking technique, you can achieve the walking speed necessary to reach or exceed 8 kilometers per hour (12-minute miles, or 5 miles per hour), which burns more calories than jogging without any unpleasant concussion and risk of injury. We are going counter to our main goal if we run instead of walk faster for exercise. We do not want efficiency; we want to burn calories in a way that is sustainable, natural, and injury free.

For you to walk at an aerobic speed to lose weight and get fit, you must understand that the speed needed is *beyond* the point at which nature will instinctively signal you to run. It is at this juncture that walking, using the mechanical pendulum forces, becomes more work and burns more calories than the springlike elastic action of running. Here's where the walker wins. Professor Taylor calls this an "extended gait."

An interesting comparison was drawn by Professor Taylor and Professor Donald F. Hoyt in a study called "Gait and the Energetics of Locomotion in Horses." By training horses to walk and trot beyond their normal range on a motorized treadmill, Taylor and Hoyt were able to measure their oxygen consumption as they used these extended gaits. Horses normally changed from walk to trot or trot to gallop at the point where the rate of oxygen consumption was the same in the two gaits. Professors Taylor and Hoyt determined that when the gaits were extended beyond their normal range of speeds, oxygen consumption was higher in the extended gait than that which they would normally be using. They concluded that *"horses like humans change gait and select a speed within a gait in a manner that minimizes energy consumption* [my emphasis]."

Now you know why you instinctively break into a run when you are in a hurry. You pick up speed but use less energy than if you tried to walk as fast as the speed at which you are running. This is programmed into our locomotion system. You don't have to think about it. It simply happens for us and for all animals. To understand how far the extended gait can be taken in a horse, Prakas holds the world record for the mile as a trotter in the fantastic time of 1 minute 53.4 seconds. That is faster than most horses, except thoroughbreds, can gallop at full speed. The human equivalent of the extended gait would be the racewalking indoor world record for one mile, held by an American, Tim Lewis, in the amazing time of 5 minutes 41.12 seconds —which is *much* faster than most humans can run.

In a paper titled "Walking and Running" in *American Scientist,* Professor of Zoology R. McNeill Alexander of the University of Leeds, England, explains how our evolutionary origins still link our locomotion systems to the other animal species. Comparisons between human and animal locomotion are striking. According to Professor Alexander, most mammals the size of cats and larger walk and run using the same mechanical principles as in the corresponding human gaits. A cat or horse walking is essentially similar to two people walking one behind the other. A quadrupedal mammal trotting is like two people running one behind the other. It is only in the gallop, the gait used at the highest speeds, that quadrupeds do anything fundamentally different from people. Galloping involves bending movements of the back, so that the back muscles as well as the leg muscles contribute to the power required.

We have found jogging and running for weight loss and fitness to be unsuitable long-term exercises because of the recurring injury rate. Now a comparison of the walking and running gaits through the studies of zoologists gives us another reason why running is counterproductive. It doesn't use as much fat-burning energy as walking faster. The zoologists' studies clearly demonstrate that all animals, quadrupeds and bipeds, minimize energy consumption in their fastest gait of running. This is further confirmed by the chart on page 34, which shows that a human walking uses significantly more energy than a human running when their speeds exceed 12-minute miles.

With all of the technological advances humans have made over other animal species through millions of years of evolution, the zoologists have shown that our physical locomotion systems are still essentially the same as theirs. Where we differ, and what contributes to a major part of our weight problem, is that we have invented mechanical locomotion systems (automobiles, escalators, tractors, golf carts) to eliminate or greatly reduce the basic gait that all animals still use and that Cro-Magnon man used 100 percent of the time: walking. And reduced energy expenditure ultimately translates into unwanted fat. To compound the problem, many exercise physiologists have recommended jogging and running, which lead to frequent injury, since our musculoskeletal systems are not suited for prolonged running. Injury makes us inactive again—which brings us full circle, back to sedentary.

The natural gait that evolution has given us, that is injury free, to be used as often as needed, for as long as needed, day in and day out, from our infancy to our grave, is walking. Walking is so natural and has been a part of our lives for so long that we take it for granted. We spend an inordinate amount of time and money trying to find some exotic form of exercise or exercise equipment to replace nature's oldest exercise—truly a classic case of not being able to see the forest for the trees.

Although walking is our oldest and most natural exercise, as you attempt to accelerate your walk beyond your normal speed into what Professor Taylor calls an extended gait so that you can achieve a maximum aerobic level of exercise, you will be bumping up against your natural instinct to break into a run—that is, to change gait. Your legs and muscles will literally be screaming at you, "Run, dummy, it's easier!" And they're right. Your forty-thousand-year-old Cro-

Magnon musculoskeletal system doesn't know you're trying to burn off fat. It only knows that all animals normally need speed for fight or flight and that you are locked in the wrong gear. It's at this point that if you learn to accelerate and walk faster, using the proper biomechanical techniques explained in the next chapter, you will be doing the perfect exercise.

Although it is not commonly known, a walker who walks at a 12-minute-per-mile pace or faster will achieve the same aerobic training effect as joggers or runners without any of their risks of injury. A critical part of my research for this book was to prove what level of aerobic fitness could actually be achieved by someone over forty (or any other age) by merely walking.

My first trip to the Cooper Clinic was November 13, 1984. At that time, Dr. Boyd Lyles conducted a complete physical and fitness examination. It was the most thorough I have ever had, and is now an annual event. At that November examination, I lasted 26 minutes on the stress test with a heartbeat of 178. That gave me a superior fitness level of a male aged thirty to thirty-nine. Dr. Lyles was impressed and I was surprised. I had only been walking six or eight months after my knee gave out from jogging. I walked in the conventional manner and had managed to do five miles in one hour a few times. But mostly I walked the five miles at a 12½-to-13-minute-per-mile pace simply because that was all I could muster using a normal arm swing and a normal parallel stride.

When I left the Cooper Clinic that November day, I

wondered if my fitness would improve even more if I really knew how to walk fast. My curiosity about the possible fitness benefits from fast walking was truly aroused. The very next day, I began a search to find out all I could about how to walk fast, *properly.* Fortunately, fate and circumstances led me to two top walking experts, Larry Young and Leonard Jansen, who provided the technical advice for the chapter on aerobic walking that follows. They taught me the race-walking technique so that I could consistently walk at a 12-minute-per-mile pace or faster.

After three months of walking my regular five-mile course at a 10-to-12-minute-per-mile pace, with an occasional speedwork thrown in, I called Dr. Lyles at the Cooper Clinic for a recheck of my fitness, which took place June 3, 1985. My stress test time increased to 28 minutes and 32 seconds and it was done with a heartbeat of 173, five ticks *lower* than before. The increased time and lowered heartbeat indicated I had truly increased my cardiovascular fitness without doing anything more dramatic than walking faster. Not to be overlooked, my percentage of body fat had dropped from 18 to 13 and my weight from 189 to 178. For my height of six feet two inches, the weight and low percentage of body fat indicated that this fifty-nine-year-old guy with two gimpy legs was dead fit.

It is significant to note also that my first fitness test was rated superior for a much younger age range (30 to 39) than my own. As every exercise physiologist knows, making incremental improvement from the high fitness level I already had did not come easily. Will aerobic walking work for everybody *exactly* as it did for me? I believe it will, but whether aerobic walking will produce the exact same fitness results for everybody is not the point. What is important is that when all the other exercises and all aspects of exercise are considered, *none will produce results any better.* Many exercises do not produce the kind of aerobic benefits you need at all. No other readily available exercise gives you a better return on time invested than aerobic walking.

At the Cooper Clinic, aerobic fitness is tested on the "Cooper Clinic modified Balke protocol." You start walking at 3.3 miles per hour on a level treadmill (without holding on to anything) for the first minute. Then the treadmill elevates 2 percent at the second minute and 1 percent for each additional minute until twenty-five minutes have passed. At the end of twenty-five minutes, the treadmill is tilted so that you are walking up a 25 percent grade (a fourteen-degree incline). That's steep! The speed is then increased .2 mile per hour each minute until you are exhausted—that is, if you aren't before this. Fifteen electrodes are attached to your chest and upper body to monitor your ECG. Blood pressure and pulse are constantly checked.

As I mentioned earlier, the Cooper Clinic has conducted over eighty thousand of these elaborate tests on men and women and has perhaps the most extensive stress test experience of any single medical source in the world. With this enormous background of medical data, Dr. Cooper has constructed a definition-of-fitness chart for men and women based on age ranges and times established on the stress test (see page 42).

My stress test time of 28 minutes and 32 seconds

exceeded the "Superior" fitness aerobic capacity of a man thirty years or younger, as shown on the chart. Dr. Boyd Lyles was so impressed with my performance that he had the clinic's publications department do an article with pictures of the aerobic walking technique. It appeared in the July 1985 issue of *Aerobics*, published by the Cooper Clinic. On the cover of that same

DEFINITION OF FITNESS CATEGORIES FOR MALES

Age Group (years)

FITNESS CATEGORY	<30	30–39	40–49	50–59	60+
☐ ***Very Poor***	<14:59	<13:09	<11:59	<9:59	<6:59
☐ ***Poor***	15:00–17:29	13:10–15:59	12:00–14:14	10:00–12:06	7:00– 9:99
☐ ***Fair***	17:30–20:59	16:00–19:59	14:15–17:59	12:07–15:39	10:00–13:21
☐ ***Good***	21:00–23:59	20:00–22:59	18:00–20:59	15:40–18:59	13:22–16:59
☐ ***Excellent***	24:00–26:59	23:00–25:59	21:00–24:29	19:00–22:14	17:00–20:55
☐ ***Superior***	27:00+	26:00+	24:30+	22:15+	20:56+

DEFINITION OF FITNESS CATEGORIES FOR FEMALES

Age Group (years)

FITNESS CATEGORY	<30	30–39	40–49	50–59	60+
☐ ***Very Poor***	<9:59	<8:59	<7:19	<5:59	<4:59
☐ ***Poor***	10:00–12:16	9:00–11:08	7:20– 9:59	6:00– 7:42	5:00– 6:15
☐ ***Fair***	12:17–15:29	11:09–14:09	10:00–12:29	7:43–10:13	6:16– 8:59
☐ ***Good***	15:30–18:59	14:10–17:29	12:30–15:34	10:14–12:52	9:00–11:59
☐ ***Excellent***	19:00–21:59	17:30–19:59	15:35–17:59	12:53–15:06	12:00–15:33
☐ ***Superior***	22:00+	20:00+	18:00+	15:07+	15:34+

issue was Tatu, the Portuguese twenty-three-year-old "superstar for the Dallas Sidekicks of the Major Indoor Soccer League." His time for the same stress test was 27 minutes and 45 seconds. With all the running soccer players do, one would assume their fitness level would be hard to beat. Pardon me while I brag a little, but this old walker—with two screws in his right knee and no cartilage on the medial side—spotted the young soccer player thirty-four years in age and beat him by 47 seconds.

In case anybody might think that was a fluke, the December 1985 issue of *Aerobics* had three rookie basketball players for the Dallas Mavericks of the NBA on the cover. All three had just had their fitness and cardiovascular levels checked on a treadmill at the Cooper Clinic. They were tested on the "Bruce Protocol." Comparable time on the Balke test that I took is calculated by multiplying their time by 1.7. The number one draft choice, forward-guard Detlef Schrempf, lasted 25 minutes and 30 seconds at the converted Balke stress test time before, as he put it, "My lungs gave out." "I couldn't breathe," said Schrempf, who played for the University of Washington and was a member of the 1984 West German Olympic team. Seven-foot forward-center Bill Wennington, who played at St. John's University and was a member of the 1984 Canadian Olympic team, lasted 23 minutes 14 seconds on the Balke treadmill equivalent. Uwe Blab, the seven-foot-two-inch center from Indiana University, and also a member of the West German Olympic team, had the best time of 27 minutes 12 seconds.

These three NBA professional basketball players in their early twenties and near-midseason form, failed to beat my time of 28 minutes and 32 seconds, and a couple of them didn't even get close.

The treadmill is an impartial judge. It doesn't know and doesn't care how old you are, what kind of exercise or sport you have engaged in, what your sex is, or what your athletic ability is. It tests everybody the same. How fast each person reaches the terminal point of exhaustion establishes his or her level of cardiovascular fitness. Why a fifty-nine-year-old noncompetitive walker with a couple of bum legs like me could outlast professional athletes more than thirty years younger on a stress test treadmill raises an interesting question. Is the fitness exercise I am doing superior to the running and fitness exercises they are doing? Maybe so. What is truly significant for anyone reading this, however, is that I achieved the "Superior" level of fitness of a person thirty years of age or younger by simply walking aerobically. I do not racewalk competitively. I walk only for fitness and weight control, and it works sensationally.

How would world-class walkers stack up versus world-class runners in a stress test for aerobic fitness? In the summer of 1977, at the Olympic training camp in Squaw Valley, California, Larry Young, who won the bronze medal at the 1968 and 1972 Olympic games in the 50K (31.1 miles) racewalk, was given a treadmill stress test. He was in training at the time for the racewalking world championship races to be held that year in Sheffield, England. Young told me that the attending physicians informed him that Frank Shorter, who won the United States' first gold medal in the marathon at the 1972 Olympic games in Munich, held the best stress test time of all the Olympic athletes. Larry Young's stress test that day was second only to Shorter's. While this means a marathon runner had the highest aerobic fitness capacity, it took no less than a legend to beat the walker. Think of how many other Olympic runners finished behind Larry Young, the walker.

Further evidence of aerobic capacity of walkers compared to runners was established in an article entitled "Characteristics of National Class Racewalkers" in the September 1981 issue of *The Physician and Sportsmedicine.* It states, "Physiological and selected psychological characteristics of nine highly trained racewalkers were studied and the results compared to those for distance runners and other athletes of similar age." The evaluations included body composition, physical work capacity, blood chemistry, and pulmonary function. The summary stated, "With the exception of a slightly lower aerobic capacity [notice they only said "slightly"] *the physiological and psychological profile of the racewalker is indeed similar to that of the marathon runner* [my emphasis]." The facts are: Walking can help you achieve maximum aerobic fitness compared to running and jogging at the fifty-nine-year-old-hacker level like me, at the world-class level like Larry Young, an Olympic medalist, or at the national-class level. But it's at all levels. The effectiveness of aerobic walking and racewalking is the most overlooked, underrated aspect of the physical fitness boom. For injury-free results, these exercises stand alone.

When considering aerobic conditioning, most exercise physiologists wouldn't mention cross-country skiing and walking in the same breath. On the other hand, I have found that most exercise physiologists don't really comprehend walking's aerobic exercise potential. I firmly believe a comparison of cross-country skiing to the extended gait of aerobic walking and racewalking is not only valid but is also important in order to elevate the recognition of walking to the status it deserves.

It was our unheralded Olympic racewalking medalist, Larry Young, who drew the comparison for me. Young said that many of this European racewalking acquaintances used cross-country skiing for conditioning and as a crossover sport. Conversely, in Europe, a number of Nordic cross-country skiers use racewalking in the off-season to stay in condition because it uses the upper and lower body in a strenuous, rhythmic, concussion-free movement similar to cross-country skiing. Young told me he has always regretted that he was not exposed to cross-country skiing until his competitive days were over. He would like to have attempted to compete in both events, because he felt they complemented each other so well.

One of the reasons cross-country skiing is so effective aerobically is that the skier is locked into a single unnatural, inefficient man-made gait. After all, man was not born with long, skinny slats on his feet and poles dangling off the ends of his arms. When we hook those on ourselves, we eliminate the option of nature's most efficient gait, running. It's like driving a car with only one gear. To go faster all the skier can do is struggle within the confines of the equipment. The only way he can accelerate is by developing a rhythmic kick, stride, and glide with the legs while coordinating a poling action with the upper body and arms. This means the skier is literally locked into one gear—and not an efficient gear at that. It takes a lot of effort to move along rapidly.

The aerobic walker and the racewalker lock into the walking gait, and by using a rhythmic hip-and-leg movement in synchronization with vigorous coordinated pumping of the arms can achieve phenomenal speed and concussion-free, aerobic benefit similar to the cross-country skier. In fact, tests of the aerobic level of world-class racewalkers, cross-country skiers, and marathoners all compare favorably. Aerobic walking requires considerable mental concentration because the temptation to break into the cheaper-energy gait of running is a natural instinct you have to fight until you fully develop your leg muscles and walking technique. Because the cross-country skier knows that running is physically impossible, it does not present a temptation.

Incapacitating concussion-type injuries are nonexistent in both events because the participants are pulling against nature's constant and correct force, gravity, with one foot always on the ground. Cross-country skiing and aerobic walking are similar to running a five-speed sports car at high speed in third gear. The engine labors harder, and you'll burn more fuel than if you shifted into the most efficient, fifth gear. But isn't that what we want to do: work the muscles harder and burn more calories? By now, you must be asking yourself, "If walking is as good as you claim, why isn't it more widely recommended as an aerobic exercise?" What follows are just a few examples of why walking is probably the best-kept aerobic exercise secret in this country.

A couple of years ago, when I realized my knees and legs would no longer take the punishment of jogging, I was on the edge of panic. The combination of jogging and diet modification had given me weight control and an energy level I had not experienced in thirty years, and I certainly didn't want to lose these. Apprehensively, I started my search for an alternative exercise. At the Waldenbooks store in St. Joseph, I headed for the health and fitness section. One book caught my eye right away, *The Complete Book of Walking*, by a nationally recognized physical fitness expert and the editors of *Consumer Guide*. I soon found out that it and the several other walking books I tried after that were all woefully incomplete and riddled with misinformation. *Consumer Guide*'s advice on walking was not complete in any sense of the word. The chapter advising how to walk claims: "Our Proven Method Enables You to Get the Most from Every Walk." Not true. The initial instruction states, "Here is *Consumer Guide* magazine's advice: Walk naturally." They also advise, "Don't exaggerate your arm motion. Allow your arms to hang loosely at your sides. They will swing in the opposite direction of your legs." I wonder if the people at *Consumer Guide* believe that there are people who walk with their arms swinging in the same direction as their legs? *Consumer Guide* then reminds us that "each foot should strike the ground at your heel." That may be helpful for people who walk on their tiptoes. The final bit of advice is, "Don't follow these guidelines slavishly. It's likely that the way you walk already is best for you." When I finished that sentence, I felt like singing Peggy Lee's old standard, "Is That All There Is?"

One book, *Dietwalk—The Doctor's Fast and Easy 3-Day Superdiet*, promises increased aerobic training, improved circulation, and a higher level of energy after six weeks of a walking program. So far so good. But at the bottom of the same page, the doctor goes on to say, "The speed of walking should be between 2½ and 3½ miles per hour since walking is a moderate type exercise." Well, the doctor can't have it both ways. If we're going to get the "aerobic training" he mentions at the top of the page, we won't get it at 2½ or 3½ miles per hour, unless we are five feet tall and weigh three hundred pounds, in which case, tying our shoelaces is probably "aerobic."

It was also surprising to find that the President's Council on Physical Fitness and Sports doesn't understand the true potential of walking, either. I wrote to the Government Printing Office in Washington, D.C., and secured their booklet "Walking." The writers recommend that you work toward an eventual goal where you can comfortably walk three miles in forty-five minutes. For someone who is really in sad shape and hasn't exercised in years, the President's Fitness Council recommendation is a good *interim* goal, but certainly not the *eventual* goal. We are all capable of doing more walking and faster walking than we realize.

When "faster" is introduced into the picture, however, all the physical fitness experts, including the President's Council on Physical Fitness, seem to believe running is the only alternative. For a comparison, I also got the government's booklet "Running." It lists the many healthful reasons to run; then it advises those who are truly out of shape to start out walking. Everybody seems to concede that walking works up to a point. The President's Council on Fitness then advises, "If you can comfortably walk three miles in forty-five minutes, it's okay to start running."

The seemingly uncontrollable fascination with running as a superior exercise never lets up. The director of program development for the President's Council on Physical Fitness was quoted in an article in the *Orlando Sentinel* as saying, "The beauty of walking is that a lot of people will want to go beyond that. It's a natural progression to running or jogging." His obvious bias prompts me to remind readers that the only thing running and jogging can give you that you don't get from aerobic walking is *injury.* When *Consumer Guide,* members of the medical profession, and the U.S. government can't seem to get it right on what is possible with a good, strong walking program, is it any wonder that aerobic walking is the best-kept exercise secret in this country?

The bottom line is this: There isn't any exercise or exercise equipment that has curative powers or that can produce miraculous results. They only provide the means by which we can rhythmically exercise the major muscle groups in the upper and lower body (preferably simultaneously) to elevate the heart rate into the aerobic training range, while at the same time expending caloric energy in an effort to get rid of unwanted fat. That is absolutely all any of them can do, including walking. It requires a considerable amount of sustained physical activity to achieve the desired results, no matter what exercise you do. Whether you want to believe it or not, there is no effortless way.

You can get all the desired exercise results from running, but you're exposed to an unacceptable risk of injury. A few pieces of exercise equipment will produce aerobic results at the price of unsustainable, mind-numbing boredom. Swimming, cycling, and other exercises all have some merit but also many offsetting limitations. Cross-country skiing is an enjoyable, injury-free exercise that has it all, but it is totally inaccessible for at least 90 percent of the people because of geography and the unavailability of snow. Only walking, if done properly, can produce *all* of the desired exercise results and is available at any place at any time. It is the only exercise backed by over four million evolutionary years of injury-free use.

If you would like to lose weight permanently and get

in good physical shape but are continually stymied, no matter what you try, then you are a prime candidate for nature's oldest and most successful exercise: walking. All you need to know now is how to walk aerobically.

4. THE PERFECT EXERCISE— AEROBIC WALKING

This chapter gives you the specifics of how to walk aerobically. Misinformation from exercise physiologists, most of whom rate walking as a "moderate to light exercise" and not one that will produce a high-level aerobic training effect, has created an enormous exercise gap that has left millions who sorely need a sustainable, injury-free, aerobic exercise stranded on the sidelines. Now you will learn how to bridge that gap with the most current biomechanical information on aerobic walking available. This information comes from Larry Young and Leonard Jansen, who taught me.

They are two of the best sources possible, and they have provided all of the technical walking information for this book.

Larry Young, our only Olympic racewalking medalist at the current distances, won twenty-five national titles during a record-smashing career that brought world-class status to American racewalking in a sport dominated by the Europeans and the Mexicans. Young won a gold medal in the 50K walk (31.1 miles) at the 1967 Pan-American games, setting a new record. He won his first Olympic bronze in 1968 at Mexico City. In 1972 at the Olympics in Munich, Young won the 50K bronze again in one of the toughest fields of walkers ever assembled. The first five finishers all bettered the existing world record. Young walked the 31.1-mile course at an average of 7 minutes and 43 seconds per mile to take the bronze behind a West German and a Russian.

Leonard Jansen was the 1976 New Jersey AAU 20K running champion. He turned to racewalking because of an Achilles tendon injury. Jansen obtained his masters degrees in mathematics and computer science from Penn State University, and he now heads up computer services of the Sports Science Division at our fine United States Olympic Committee (USOC) headquarters in Colorado Springs. Leonard Jansen was an invaluable source for research material and consultation. As an analyst at the biomechanics lab at USOC headquarters, he has viewed and analyzed literally miles of film and videotape on the top world-class walkers from the Russians and East Germans to the

Mexican 1984 Olympic 20K and 50K gold medalists. Jansen is probably the foremost authority in the United States on the current state of the art of world-class racewalking. The biomechanical technique you will be learning in order to walk aerobically is essentially the same technique used by the world-class racewalkers.

Let's start by restating the difference between aerobic walking and racewalking. It is nothing more than the speed of the walker. Both will produce an aerobic effect, but racewalking takes you up to competitive race speed. It is identical to the difference between jogging and running. Someone who is twenty pounds or more overweight and who has not exercised aggressively for many years may find that he or she is walking aerobically at a 20-minute mile or slower. That is, the heart rate is up in the 70 to 85 percent training range. How do you find the 70 to 85 percent training range? Just take your pulse and then do a little simple arithmetic. To calculate your cardiorespiratory range, simply take 220, subtract your age, and then figure 70 to 85 percent of that number. For instance, the lower rate of the training range for a fifty-year-old would be 119 ($220 - 50 = 170$; $70 \times 170 = 119$). If you are fifty years old and exercise strongly enough to raise your pulse to 119, you will be at 70 percent of your "cardiorespiratory capacity."

The greatest risk to an overweight, out-of-shape person is doing too much, too soon. Monitoring your heart rate by taking your pulse will prevent that. Anybody who has driven a sports car knows there's a "red line" on the tachometer as a warning not to allow the engine's RPMs (revolutions per minute) to go above a certain level and risk blowing the engine. You can monitor the "RPMs" of your heart by checking your pulse. According to most doctors, your cardiorespiratory "red line" is 85 percent of capacity. Above that, you are exercising in the danger zone. For a fifty-year-old person 85 percent would be 144. To make consistently good progress, it is best to aim for the 70 to 85 percent range. If you can keep your pulse within that range, you will be doing all that's necessary.

For an out-of-shape, over-forty person starting out from a fat, sedentary standstill, it will not take much exercise to pump the heart rate up over the 70 percent rate. That's OK if you don't have chest pains and can handle it comfortably. Checking your pulse rate is absolutely essential to measuring your progress and to making sure you are reaching an aerobic level. As time goes by, you will find you can handle more and more exercise before your heart rate hits 70 percent or more. That's a sure sign you are getting fit. Incidentally, a simple way to get your pulse count is to take your pulse for fifteen seconds and multiply by four. For instance, if your pulse rate was 30 for fifteen seconds, then for a full minute it would be 120 (multiplying by four). This method might not be quite as accurate as if you counted for the full sixty seconds, but a few ticks one way or the other won't matter. The computations on the chart opposite show the heart rate training ranges.

Memorize your range of 70 to 85 percent. Know

where that 85 percent "red line" is at all times and stay below it. It is extremely important that you know exactly what your heart rate training range is, particularly in the early stage of your exercise program when being overweight and out of shape can put a strain on the cardiovascular system that it isn't prepared to handle. The pulse normally drops quickly when exercise is stopped, so take your pulse just as you are slowing down to get a reasonably accurate count. If your pulse stays high for ten or fifteen minutes after you've stopped exercising, you probably should consult your doctor.

AGE	25	30	35	40	45	50	55	60	65	70	75	80
70%	136	133	129	126	122	119	116	112	109	105	102	98
85%	166	161	157	153	149	144	140	136	132	128	123	119

You shouldn't try to hit the 70 to 85 percent training range on day one. In fact, I believe anyone who is more than twenty pounds overweight (from their best weight in their early twenties) and has not exercised regularly for a number of years should stay in the 50 to 65 percent range for the first thirty days until they develop a minimal amount of fitness and get over some initial muscle soreness. Remember, this is to be a lifetime commitment, so there's no big hurry to try to achieve magical results in a short period of time. Hopefully, by now you accept the fact that that is not possible. As you continue to walk farther and get fitter, it will be necessary to walk faster to keep your heart in the training range. Over time, this will require you to keep pushing yourself to maintain a higher level of speed. Using the racewalking technique will permit you to accomplish this.

You will have to learn how to pass beyond that instinctive desire to break into a run. You will have to walk at the extended gait. In order to ultimately achieve the speed of 12-minute miles or faster, it will be necessary to make some basic changes in the manner in which you walk. These biomechanical changes will help you develop a fluid, rhythmic movement to gain the speed level needed. I don't want anyone to get intimidated by world-class walkers' speed any more than a jogger should be intimidated by world-class runners' speed. You only need to walk as far and as fast as necessary to burn off the fat, get fit, and feel good. For those who want to go on to competitive speeds, the sky is the limit. I confidently predict that you'll feel stronger than an acre of garlic if you'll just hang in there and push yourself into the extended gait. Actually, you are tougher than you think you are. The problem is, you are also softer than you thought you were.

The question arises immediately: How much should I walk? Many of the exercise books I reviewed had elaborate schedules laid out for days, weeks, and months. I was never sure if it was actually necessary to be so rigid or if the author just needed filler for the book. If five hundred people of various backgrounds took a basic written test of mental capacity, there would be a great variety of results, such as superior, excellent, good, average, poor, and failure. It makes sense that if the same five hundred people took a fitness-level test, they would have similar wide-ranging results. To start everybody out at the same level could result in wasting time for those who are in the top third and might be injurious and discouraging to those in the bottom 10 percent. Everyone is different, and we should proceed with our exercise on that basis.

Your body is constantly sending you signals about its condition. From this point forward, your observance of and curiosity about your body and how it is "talking" to you becomes extremely important. You *must* be able to know if you are doing too little or too much. The amount of exercise we should do was described best by Dr. Sheehan in the May 1985 issue of *The Runner* magazine. He wrote, "The body is the best training guide. It will tell you how far to go, how fast, how often. It will decide, if you listen, about smoking and diet, on alcohol and stress management. It will tell you when to push and when to coast. When to reach for a peak and when to remain in peace and quiet."

In effect, he is telling us that our individual bodies determine our individual schedules. Do all you can every day, knowing that some days will be better than others. But aren't they anyway, whether you exercise or not? Remember, you are simply trying to recapture the weight and fitness level you had when you were in your early twenties. There is no timetable except the one your body can realistically handle when you push it to perform. Dr. Sheehan, who is in his late sixties, has a beautiful way with words in describing his personal level of fitness. He says, "The body has a mind of its own. Mine is telling me that I am no particular age. I am an athlete capable of infinitely more activity than I have suspected. The difference between my body in my thirties and forties and fifties and now may be detected through the use of sophisticated physiological tests. It is not apparent to me in operation."

Dr. Sheehan is a man of unusual discipline and durability. His fitness level was obtained through running. You can achieve a similar high level of fitness and personal satisfaction by learning to walk aerobically. When I started out to jog five years ago (at a pace much slower than I now *walk*!), I could not do a continuous half mile. I was seeing white dots darting around in front of my eyes, had a burning in the chest and a stabbing pain in the side, coupled with a light-headed sensation. It was a terrible revelation of my condition, but I can look back now and smile. In time, you can too.

To measure your current status and future progress, you will need an exercise route of known distance. Take your car and measure out a two-mile course in your neighborhood with the odometer. Or if you know how many city blocks to a mile, that's just as good. Know where the half-mile marks are. I am fortunate to be able to walk a course of lightly traveled country roads that form a five-mile rectangle. But I know that the red barn is a half mile and the blue silo is a mile, and so forth. This way you can time yourself initially to see how *long* it takes to walk a mile or two, and later to find out how *fast* you can walk that same distance.

I have taught several hundred men and women how to walk aerobically at our local YMCA clinics. Most people who come to the clinics are already doing some walking, but few of them know exactly how far or how fast they are going. I have found this to be a universal fault of most walkers. On the other hand, practically all the joggers or runners can tell you how far they go and how many minutes per mile it takes them. Most of them know what their heart training range is and if they are hitting it. Remember, you are not going out for a stroll; you are going out for an aerobic workout. It is absolutely essential that *each day* you know exactly the distance you walked, how many minutes per mile it took, and if you hit your heart training range and held it for twenty minutes or longer. If you miss the latter, you're not pushing hard enough and you will not get the results you are looking for. If you're just starting out, you should find out how long it takes you to walk a flat mile (not uphill or downhill) comfortably. If you can go only a half mile without great stress, then that's all you've got. You at least know what your starting capacity is and you can build from there. Measuring your progress each day gives you motivation to keep improving.

The ultimate goal is to get to a level of fitness where you can crank off three miles in a *minimum* of 36 minutes any time you want to. Once you reach that level, you will be burning more calories than a jogger and you'll develop an aerobic fitness better than a jogger's. At least I did. Your overall body fitness will exceed that of the jogger because you will be working harder and using upper-body muscles not used in jogging. The total involvement of the lower-body muscles in aerobic walking also exceeds that of jogging. You'll be pleasantly surprised to know that once you reach the three-miles-in-36-minutes level, you can just as easily increase your distance to four or five miles if you want to burn more calories. My wife, Carol, and I know that we need five miles, five or six days a week, to eat without dieting. You'll probably find, as we did, that walking is more enjoyable and much easier than dieting. Two miles in 24 minutes should give you a pretty good aerobic fitness, but you may have to add some miles to that to hold your weight where you want it. Be prepared to walk a lot of miles during your weight-reduction period. This is the critical period when you must burn considerably more calories than you are taking in. There is no other way. Once you acheive your weight goal, you should be able to walk less and maintain your desired weight by eating smart without dieting. Everyone is different, so you will have to experiment to find out what your metabolic system needs.

FOUR STRETCHES TO GET YOU READY

I have made every blunder possible in developing a livable, workable, effective exercise schedule. I was a typical overweight, out-of-shape guy who frankly dreaded the thought of exercise, so I took every shortcut I could. One of my dumbest mistakes was walking for almost a year and jogging for three years without ever doing any muscle-stretching and flexibility exercises. Some exercise books put those in the back, and I felt they must not be very important. Wrong! I found them extremely important in walking, more so than in jogging. That's why I am giving them to you first. Larry Young, our Olympic racewalking medalist, says, "Stretching should improve your flexibility, but equally important, stretching exercises improve your coordination." During his best competitive years, Young actually took modern dance classes to increase his flexibility and rhythm. When we come to the specific technique for aerobic walking, you will see how flexibility contributes to the rhythmic movement required.

You can get by with four stretches, which only takes a few minutes. You should do them regularly before and after each walk. There are more exercises and stretches we all *should* do, but my experience is, if most people will at least do these few that affect the walking muscles and then spend their time walking, they'll do just fine. It serves no purpose to lay out an elaborate, time-consuming stretching and stationary exercise routine that will cause more people to quit than to continue.

When you are just beginning, leg-muscle stretching is absolutely essential, even on the days you don't walk. On those days you should actually try to do the stretches two or three times as long—you can do them while you're watching TV. Stretching will definitely help keep muscle tightness and soreness to a minimum. It will give you the ability to stride out and pick up your speed. The pleasant thing about these stretches is that they don't really take any great effort, just a little time. All stretches should be done with a slow, *steady* pull until you feel the muscle slightly ache. Don't induce outright sharp pain, and above all, don't bounce or snap the muscle. Think of it as if you were slowly and evenly stretching out a thick rubber band. Once you feel the low-intensity ache, hold your position for fifteen or twenty seconds and then ease off and switch to the other leg. Three repetitions per muscle are generally enough to be effective. If you have time, don't hesitate to do more. This is definitely a case where more is better.

The muscle stretches a little more on each repetition. Over a period of time, you'll be amazed at how supple those old muscles become. The four muscles to be stretched are the calf muscle, the shin muscle, the front thigh muscle, and the back thigh muscle (commonly referred to as the "hamstring").

Let's just start with the shin muscle because later on, as you pick up speed, that muscle is probably going to be barking at you pretty loud for a while. It will take some time, but it will quiet down as it gets fit. This is the most difficult muscle to exercise because there isn't any easy way to get at it.

Leonard Jansen at USOC taught me what I think is

the simplest and best shin-muscle exercise, one you can do anytime, even sitting at your desk at work.

Shin-Muscle Exercise

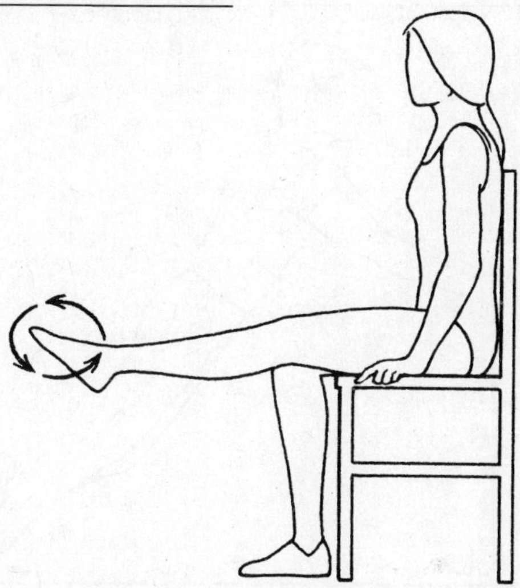

Sit in a chair and with your foot off the floor tilt your toes as far back toward your shin as you can. Then rotate your toes in a large circle. When your toes hit the bottom of the circle, 180 degrees from where they started, they'll be pointing down away from your leg. Make sure you point them down as far as possible. Make three or four big circles clockwise and then reverse and make three or four circles counterclockwise. Repeat several times. This will wake up your shin muscle and you'll feel it. If your shin muscle doesn't bother you as you increase your walking speed, you can eliminate this exercise.

Calf-Muscle and Tendon Stretch

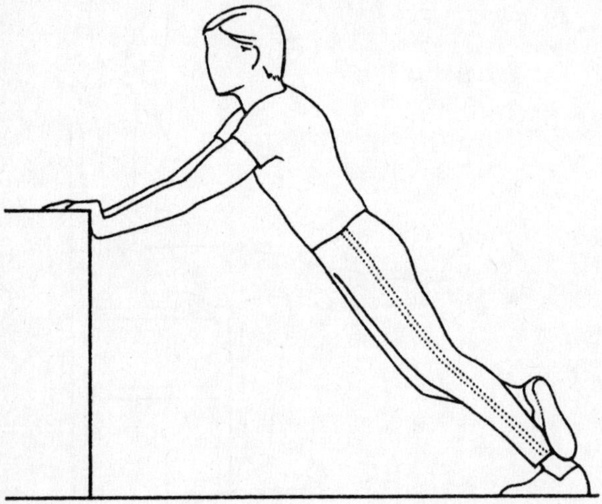

Lean against a wall or tree (I sometimes use the kitchen counter) and with one foot absolutely flat on the floor and back several feet from the wall lean forward with your hips until you feel the tension in your calf muscle. Just hook the other foot loosely over the back of the ankle of the leg you are stretching to get it out of the way. Be sure to keep the heel of your weight-bearing foot flat on the floor to get maximum stretching in the calf muscles and tendon. Alternate legs and do this three or four times on each leg for fifteen or twenty seconds at a time.

Hamstring Stretch

There are a number of ways to stretch the hamstring muscle, some of which involve bending over. I have one of those backs that pops out once in a while, and I prefer the following method; it's better than bending over. Just put your foot up on a counter, chair, or table with your leg extended. It is best if it is parallel to the floor when extended, but if it tilts down a little, that is OK. Try not to have it tilt up. Now lean forward and slide your hands down along your leg toward your ankle. Don't bounce. You will feel that big muscle up the back of your thigh pulling. This is an important muscle to stretch. The hamstring can affect the length of your stride. If you do much walking on hills, as I do, it will tend to tighten up. Do the same number of repetitions on the hamstring as you did on the calf muscles.

Front Thigh Muscle Stretch

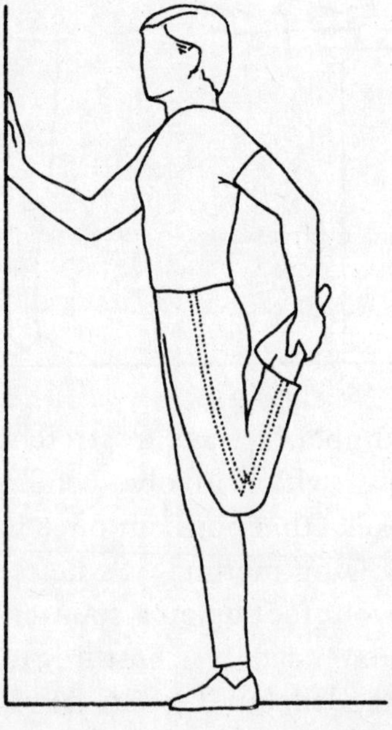

Stand next to a wall or tree for balance. Reach back and pull one foot up toward your buns slowly until you feel that dull ache on the front of your thigh. Repeat as in the other stretches. When I first did this stretch, I couldn't get my heel within six inches of my backside. Now it touches with hardly any strain. Don't try to force it too quickly. In time you should get a full stretch on this muscle, unless you have some stiffness in a knee joint (as I have in one). This might prevent getting the heel all the way up.

I urge you to do these stretches every day, whether you walk aerobically or not. They will make your muscles function better for normal everyday walking. They take only a few minutes and can be done just about anyplace, and you don't have to work up a sweat to do them. You are now ready to go out and walk.

I purposely did not give you upper-body and arm exercises to do at home with your stretches. As you walk the first hundred yards or so at an easy pace, swing your arms around like windmills, clockwise and counterclockwise. Swing them straight out in front so your hands clap and then back behind till your fingertips touch. Roll your head clockwise and counterclockwise a few times to loosen up the neck muscles. Now you are ready to roll.

CONCENTRATE ON POSTURE

The very first thing nearly everyone has to learn is correct posture. In real estate, they say the three most important things are "location, location, location." In walking, the three most important things are "posture, posture, posture"! You must walk with your shoulders back, head level, and chin up. Don't tilt your head back, or to the side, or overcorrect. The head is approximately 7 percent of the total weight of the body. The head, supported by the spinal cord, should be in an absolute neutral position, permitting relaxed neck and shoulder muscles. Tilting it forward or sideways places stress and force concentrations on the first five spinal vertebrae. Head, upper body, hip, leg, and foot placements are all interrelated and dependent on one another in proper aerobic walking.

Get your shoulders directly over your hips with your spine straight. The correct position is much like standing at attention. One of the reasons this is so important is that it permits you to breathe more easily. You are going to need lots of oxygen. Equally important as you try to walk faster, if your head is down and you have bent your back, you will tire quickly. The muscles through the shoulders and across the small of the back will give you fits. Improper posture puts improper fatiguing torque on those muscles. It is more important to walk with good posture at a slower speed than to thrash your way along at a faster speed with the wrong posture.

In our YMCA clinics, the tendency to drop the head and shoulders is the most difficult habit to break for men or women. Until you get the posture problem whipped, repeat to yourself "Hips forward, shoulders back, chin up, hips forward, shoulders back, chin up, hips forward, shoulders back, chin up." Repeat it in cadence with your steps. As you walk faster, speed it up. You will find that keeping the shoulders back is the first thing you correct. Tilting the head down is the toughest to correct. You must hold the head up and look forward when you are walking aerobically. Learn to scan the terrain ahead by dropping your eyes, not your head. Work on it. I can assure you, if I could correct my head tilting, anyone can.

Now let's learn the specific biomechanical changes necessary to achieve the extended gait of walking. Aerobic walking and racewalking involve changing the way you utilize your arms and the way you move your hips and legs. As Larry Young once said, *"Racewalking requires the flexibility of a gymnast, the grace of a dancer, and the endurance of a marathon runner."* Don't worry, you will not be required to have the endurance of a marathon runner unless you want to push yourself up to a competitive level. The 12-minute-per-mile pace is not important initially and should not be attempted by a beginner. Consequently, until you can walk at least two miles in 26 minutes, it is not actually necessary to make any changes in your hip and leg movement. That pace can be reached with arm adjustment, good posture, and constantly pushing yourself to walk a little faster and a little farther each day. As Dr. Sheehan advises, listen to your body for when to push and when to coast. Just don't get too comfortable with coasting, because in the beginning there will be some days when your cranky muscles will be trying to talk you out of walking altogether.

THE BENT-ARM SWING

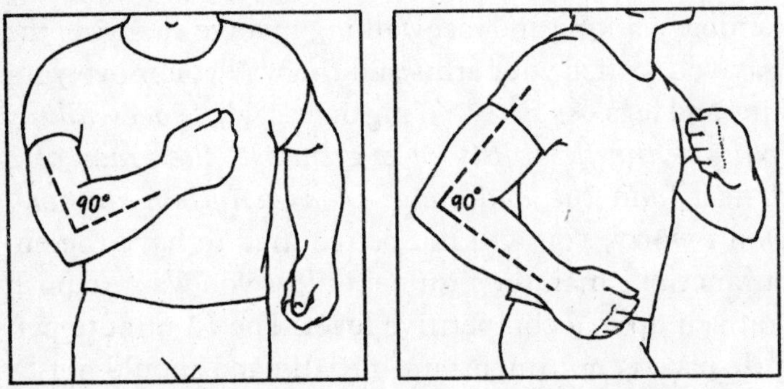

First let's learn *what* to do, and then I'll explain how it works biomechanically to help you go faster and why you might have some difficulty learning how to master it.

Bend your arms so they form 90-degree angles at the elbows. Let your arms swing loosely from the shoulder like two pendulums (which they are when you are walking). Move your arms back and forth in coordination with your steps just as if they were fully extended and hanging down at your side. The arm on the backswing should come back to where your wrist is at the centerline of your hip. The arm on the forward swing should come forward until the wrist is at the centerline of the rib cage in front. The hand should not go higher than the opposite breast on the forward swing. Form a comfortable, loose fist with your hand. On the complete arm swing from back to front the angle at the elbow should remain a constant 90 degrees. Keep shoulders squared with your line of travel. Do not permit your shoulders to swing back and forth with your arms. Your upper arm is a short pendulum swinging from your shoulder socket. That's exactly what it has become when you bent it at the elbow. As your elbow passes your rib cage on each swing, it should be close to your body, but not touching. If it is very far away from your body, you will get a flapping action and excessive shoulder movement. Let your arm hang loose and natural from your shoulder and your elbow will find the right groove to travel back and forth in.

Leonard Jansen suggests that a good way to practice the coordination of the bent-arm swing is to stand in front of a mirror and walk in place. Stand sideways to see where your wrist comes on the backswing. Develop a natural swing so that the wrist stops at the centerline of the hip. Facing the mirror, you can see your wrist as it comes to the centerline of the rib cage. Watch to make sure the follow-through on the front swing does not carry your hand higher than the opposite breast. While walking in place, coordinate your arm movement with your foot movement.

The arm is a pendulum, and when you walk, the speed at which that pendulum can complete a full swing has a direct bearing on how fast you can walk. The legs are pendulums also, and there must be synchronization between the two pendulum phases. An exaggerated swing—taking the arm too far back on the backswing or too far forward on the front swing—makes it nearly impossible to get good synchronization between the legs and arms.

Remember Professor Taylor's description of walking and running. Walking is the mechanical work of pendulums, and running involves the elastic force of muscles and tendons. When you attempt to walk as fast as possible with your arms fully extended, the long arm at the end of the backswing is a force pulling you back while the legs are trying to move you forward. You have two forces working against each other. It then becomes impossible to walk erect with good posture, and you'll find yourself leaning forward trying to overcome the long, pendular backswing of the arm.

When you bend the arms at 90 degrees, you have cut

Wrong

Correct

the length of those pendulums by more than half, and they can now swing as fast as your legs can move. Anyone who has had an old grandfather clock knows that if it is running slow, you shorten the pendulum to make it go faster.

In order to walk into the extended gait, the arms must be able to swing as fast as possible in coordination with the increased speed of the legs. There is a point at which the pendulum frequency (swinging action) of the arm when fully extended cannot complete the full swing fast enough to keep up with the legs. This may explain why many exercise books set 15-minute miles as your walking goal. They all instruct you to walk with your arms hanging down at your sides fully extended. Without biomechanically changing the arm swing, a 15-minute mile is about as fast as you can realistically expect to walk unless you lean forward and thrash around like a ruptured duck.

Don't be discouraged if you find that the simple act of bending your arms at 90 degrees and walking fast is difficult to coordinate. Quite a few people in our YMCA clinics have difficulty with this transition. Leonard Jansen has encountered the same thing and explains it this way, "The hips and legs are the propulsion unit and the arms counterbalance their movement. To do this properly, they must not be out of phase with the leg movement." As Jansen further explains, "When you shorten the pendulum [bend the arm at 90 degrees] you have to rephase the arm period of the pendulum." Look at it this way. You have spent your whole life swinging a long pendulum out of your shoulder socket and now you are swinging a short one. It has a different swing frequency and you have to put it in synchronization with your leg swing.

This transition will probably require more mental discipline than anything else you have to learn. I can't stress strongly enough how important it is to have a *complete, full-cycle (front to back, back to front) arm stroke with every step.* You will find that the front swing will be the easiest to coordinate because you can see your wrist as it comes forward to the center of the rib cage. The full backswing, however, will require the most concentration and practice. Take your wrist clear back to the centerline of your hip on each swing of the arm or you will be out of sync with your legs. This is so important that Leonard Jansen says the Olympic champion Mexican walkers spend hours at a time in their workouts concentrating on synchronizing the rhythm of the arm swing with the leg movement. Jansen says one way they do this is to set the pace of their walk with a complete rhythmic arm swing and let the legs follow. Strangely enough, they do follow. This is the reverse of normal. Try it. It is a good practice exercise to help coordinate the bent-arm swing. It works, but you will also find you cannot do it without fully concentrating on it. The biggest mistake *everybody* makes (I sure did) in this phase of aerobic walking is to make the legs go fast and let the arms just swing slightly in a namby-pamby manner. A cross-country skier can't achieve top speed without vigorous synchronized action of the legs, arms, and upper body. Neither can an aerobic walker. Work on it. It will require practice and concentration, but until you master it, you will plateau at a speed lower than you need to reach the aerobic level.

If you are truly out of shape and overweight, I suggest you postpone the bent-arm swing for at least thirty days, or until you can walk two miles in less than 30 minutes. It is best that you not have any distractions. Normal extended-arm swing will permit you to walk fast enough to develop a minimal level of fitness. The extended-gait walking speed exceeds the jog for energy and calorie expenditure at about 12-minute miles. Professor Taylor informed me that the extended gait itself starts, however, at the lower speed of about 6 kilometers per hour (16-minute miles). From a 16-minute mile up to and exceeding a 12-minute mile, the walk becomes increasingly inefficient and requires more effort. Jogging in this range is so slow that it also is inefficient and the energy expenditure difference between walking and jogging is negligible.

Perhaps you have noticed that when you are in a hurry you walk fast, then break into a little jog for a while, then go back into a walk. You may alternate back and forth several times, and neither gait seems quite right. Most likely you are in the 16-to-12-minute-mile range where the two gaits overlap. Once you approach a level of fitness where you can walk two miles in 30 minutes, then you should definitely change to the bent-arm swing. You are in the extended-gait range, and to increase speed from this point you should convert to the biomechanical arm movement that racewalkers use. It may come easily or you may have to work at it, but the bent-arm swing is necessary to help you pick up speed.

One way to prove to yourself the effectiveness of the bent-arm swing is to walk as fast as you can with your arms fully extended in a normal arm swing. While in full stride, quickly bend your arms 90 degrees and swing them in sync with your legs. Keep going for a few yards; it will seem as if you took the brakes off. You should feel a slight acceleration. Keep walking fast for a few yards more and then drop your arms back down to normal; you will immediately feel the drag and slowing effect of the extended arms as they become long pendulums again. Walking several miles a day with the arms fully extended often causes the fingers to swell as they become engorged with blood from the centrifugal force of the arm swing. Walking with the bent-arm swing eliminates this.

OVERCOMING PREDICTABLE TROUBLE SPOTS

As you become comfortable with the bent-arm swing and your overall condition improves, you should be trying to pick up speed as long as your pulse remains in the 70 to 85 percent training range. Two very predictable things will occur as you try to increase your speed, and it will take your complete concentration and discipline to counteract them. First, you will probably bend at your beltline and lean forward. This is generally accompanied by dropping the head. When you lean forward, you are subconsciously forcing yourself to walk faster to keep from literally falling on your face. As you lean, you are not working upper-body muscles properly. You transfer strain into the wrong places. You will tire easily in the muscles across the shoulders and across the lower back.

If you are going up a hill, even a small one, the muscles across the lower back will probably scream bloody murder. This is where you should remember the cadence count—hips forward, shoulders back, chin up. As soon as you straighten up and regain the proper posture, the lower-back muscles quiet down. When you get the chin up and the shoulders back in a relaxed, natural way, you'll feel the fatigue ease off up there also.

Proper posture lets you get full benefit of another one of aerobic walking's well-kept secrets. With the head and chin up, the shoulder and hips properly aligned, you get good muscle action in the abdominal area, as well as in the neck, which reduces the sagging look you might have as you burn off the fat in the double chin. It works wonders to help tighten the stomach as you burn off the spare-tire fat. That fat has to come off first, however, for you to realize how effective proper walking is in these two areas. There is no shortcut, but the walking will take care of the fat in time.

The second most predictable thing to guard against as you try to increase your overall speed is the "Frankenstein" look. I confess that it took me a while to finally eliminate this. As you walk faster, there is a great tendency to pick your shoulders up until they are right under your ear lobes. It is as if you are hunching. At the same time, your feet may want to come off the ground and do a slight jog. With the shoulders elevated out of place, we take on the look of the old Frankenstein monster. Why this is such a common occurrence in novice walkers trying to pick up speed is not known. Conditioning and practice will bring the shoulders back down into a relaxed position.

These are just a couple of predictable trouble spots you can expect as you attempt to walk farther and faster than you ever have before while learning the extended gait of aerobic walking. I can speak with great authority on mistakes, since I've made them all. There were times when I felt I had the speed and coordination of a spastic elephant. Nothing you are learning requires any particular athletic ability, however. All you need is a little perseverance and practice.

One other minor difficulty to be aware of is the initial tendency for your arms to tire in the bent-elbow position. This is generally more of a problem for women than men, although I confess I experienced some of it for the first week. It is simply a matter of strengthening the muscles that hold your arms up. The easiest thing to do is to use them until they get tired, and then lower your arms until you feel comfortable but keep right on walking. You should still have a slight angle in your arms, and they will still swing in front of you. Don't drop them to full extension if you can avoid it. Once the fatigue dissipates, pull them back up to 90 degrees. There is no need to lift weights or anything like that. An overweight, out-of-shape person has enough to do building up a good walking program.

The arm muscles will adapt in time by your simply using them in the specific way they are needed. They will strengthen through use as you are walking, while you are also using your leg muscles.

Some walkers (especially women) tend to let their hands dangle from their wrists instead of holding them up straight in line with the wrist. This creates a flapping action and can add to your arm fatigue. It also may hinder you from getting a good coordinated arm swing. Women sometimes do not feel natural carrying their hands as fists, even as loosely formed ones.

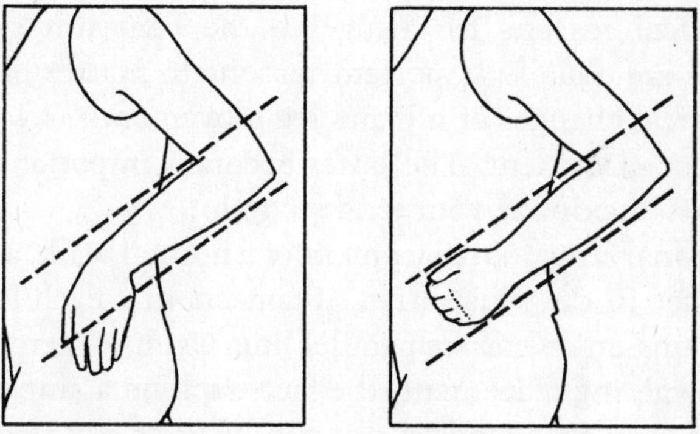

Wrong Correct

Just bending your fingers back toward the palm of your hand with the thumb barely touching the forefinger will give you a good natural look. Find any position you are comfortable with as long as the hand is held straight in line with the wrist.

LOWER-BODY MOVEMENTS

Thus far all the biomechanical attention has been from the beltline up. Once your level of fitness permits you to pump off two miles or more at about a 13-minute-per-mile pace, you are ready to make some major biomechanical changes from the beltline down. This will require your complete concentration and considerable practice. That is why I feel that changing the pendulum frequency of your arm movement should be done separately—so you won't have too many changes going on at the same time. Just as there were biomechanical reasons to change to the bent-arm swing, there are equally important reasons to master biomechanical changes of hip and leg movements as well as of foot placement. The latter becomes important as a way to maximize your stride length.

In analyzing foot placement of a normal walk, as you can see in the illustration, it appears that each foot is tracking on a separate parallel line. Using an aerobic or racewalking placement, the feet track on a single line with each foot landing directly in front of the other. Notice that the seven on-line foot placements (the same number as in the first example) covered considerably more distance.

Placing the feet on a straight line while walking

with a rapid stride cannot be done comfortably with the hips squared to your line of travel as in normal

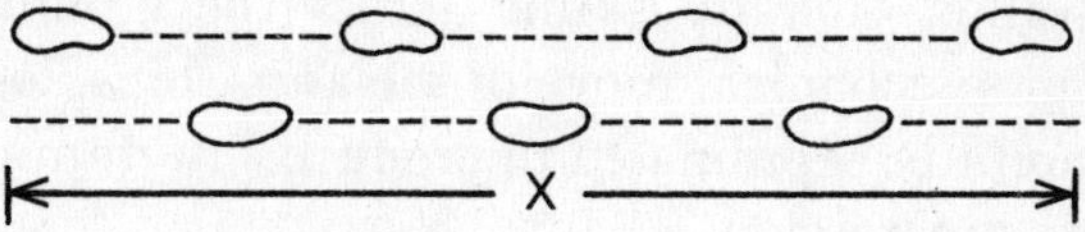

Normal Foot Placement

X = Distance Traveled

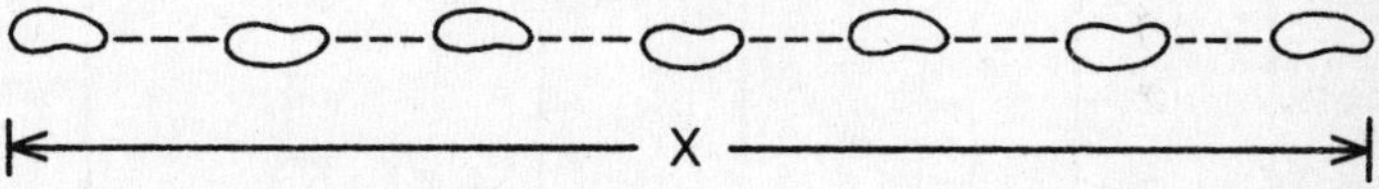

Aerobic Foot Placement

walking. To get the foot easily around and far out front for a longer stride, the hip of the leg swinging forward on each step must swivel forward with the leg swing. As your hip swivels forward, it should drop down slightly on that side so the body maintains a low center of gravity. This permits the walker to get maximum forward progression on each step. The swiveling, dropping hip action reduces wasted up-and-down motion from the high center of gravity that accompanies normal, parallel-stride walking. When your other leg swings forward, the hip on that side also swivels forward and drops down slightly, permitting the lead leg to reach out for an increased stride length. The heel should land directly in line with the toe of the back foot. Hip swivel should alternate front to back and back to front. *There should be no side-to-side wiggle.*

As each leg swings forward under the body, it should be bent at the knee just enough for the toes of the foot to clear the ground. Avoid any high-stepping action. The walker literally skims across the ground with every biomechanical move of the arms, hips, legs, and feet carefully coordinated to produce a rhythmic, fluid forward progression.

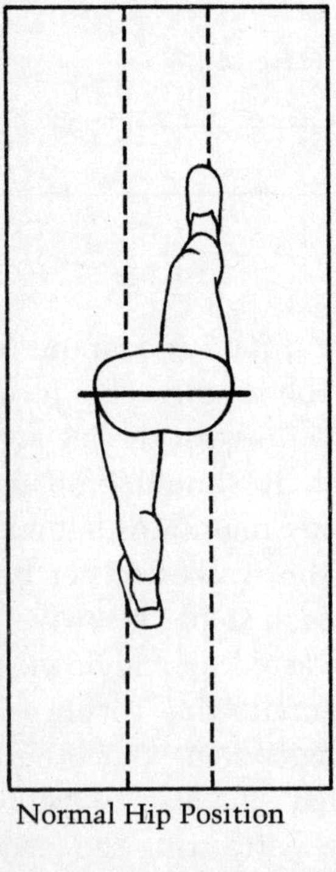

Normal Hip Position

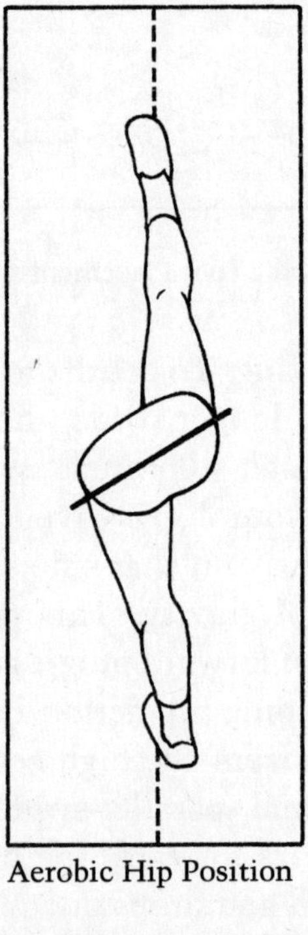

Aerobic Hip Position

This biomechanical foot placement, along with the leg swing and hip swivel, when performed with the proper posture and rhythm, permits the major muscle groups in the legs and pelvic area to power the walker along at aerobic-level speeds. Below is a cutaway view looking down on the pelvis to show how the hips should look as they swivel forward and backward with their respective leg movements.

YOU GOTTA HAVE RHYTHM

The secret to transferring this biomechanical action into aerobic walking speed is rhythm. The movement becomes a fluid, unbroken action from the beltline down. When done slowly with the head up, the shoulders back, the hips tucked directly under the shoulders, and the arms bent, the walker looks as if he or she is doing a Broadway chorus dancer's jaunty, jivin' strut. As Larry Young said, you must have the rhythm of a dancer. In fact, the best way to learn this part of aerobic walking is to approach it exactly as if you were learning a new dance step. For instance, dance instructors always have you walk slowly through the step to get the foot placement in mind. Then you attempt to increase the tempo of the step as you try to make it less mechanical and smooth it out to a rhythmic move. When you get it all together, you perform the dance at the appropriate musical tempo without even thinking about it. What started out as a cumbersome mechanical movement is now an enjoyable rhythmic reflex. That's how aerobic walking will ultimately be for you.

Through repetition and practice, the dancer's arbitrary foot placements we call dance steps make a neuromuscular imprint on the appropriate muscles. The muscles must have a sequential firing order to perform these dance steps. Once that is programmed into the brain, so it can be transmitted to the appropriate muscles in the appropriate sequence, the dancer can repeat the steps over and over without thinking about them.

To learn the biomechanical movement of aerobic walking, walk through the step slowly at first, as if you were learning a new dance. Once you get a smooth, fluid motion, pick up the tempo. If you have been able to walk at a 13-minute-per-mile pace or faster with just the bent arms and normal foot placement, be prepared to lose some speed and perhaps drop back to a 14-minute-mile pace or less when you implement the lower-body changes. This is normal while you are going through a coordinating phase. The changed arm movement, the changed foot, leg, and hip movements, making sure your posture is right, and developing a smooth-looking dancer's rhythm all take time. You will need some practice to put the new biomechanical movements all together. As in dancing, you will have to teach your muscles the right firing order.

Up until now we have been dwelling on biomechanical changes, but I can't emphasize enough that from this point forward *rhythm is the key to aerobic walking*. Any guy or gal who is a good dancer has the edge on learning aerobic walking. That may explain why it took me a while to catch on. I can't dance a lick. Carol, my wife, walked circles around me for the first month.

I would guess that Shirley MacLaine, Gene Kelly, or chorus dancers on Broadway could pick up the rhythm of aerobic walking in five minutes. They might not be fast initially, but they sure would be smooth.

UPHILL WALKING

Once you have mastered aerobic walking on level ground, you may want to increase the intensity of your walking workout by trying some hills. This requires a few biomechanical adjustments to compensate for the incline. First, you should shorten your stride length. Do not try to reach *up* the hill with your lead leg by using the same length of stride you would use on the flat. When you shorten your stride you will have to take more steps to maintain your speed, but don't worry if you lose some speed going uphill. You will soon find out that the added work involved in lifting your body up the hill, even at a slower speed, will keep your heart rate in the training range and your lungs demanding more oxygen. You will also find that your leg muscles are working harder—especially those at the front of your thighs.

Just as in walking on the flat, the most important consideration for walking uphill is good posture. Don't lean into the hill by bending your back. That would cause lower back muscle fatigue. Keep the body erect and compensate for the incline by bending at the ankles and shortening your stride. On hills that are steeper than 6 or 7 degrees, it will probably be too difficult for you to maintain good body posture and a rhythmic stride. Avoid them. Remember, there is a distinct difference in purpose and style between aerobic walking uphill and hiking up a mountain. There are some gentle rolling hills on the country roads that Carol and I walk. We like them because they help increase the intensity of our daily walks. After you have developed the fluid, rhythmic style of aerobic walking and think you are pretty fit, try some hills. They'll be a new challenge for you and they will help you increase your fitness even more.

REFINING YOUR TECHNIQUE

There are a number of other subtle specifics that must be implemented with the basic lower-body movements we have just discussed. A knowledge of the rules of racewalking, even though most of you don't intend to enter a race, is important so you will know what you should do to develop the proper technique. Rhythm coupled with technique will ultimately permit you to develop a smooth aerobic level of speed.

According to the rule book of The Athletics Congress of the U.S.A., "Racewalking is a progression of steps so taken that unbroken contact with the ground is maintained. The lead foot must touch the surface before the back foot leaves the ground. During each stride, the leg must be straightened (e.g., not bent at the knee) for at least one moment, the supporting leg

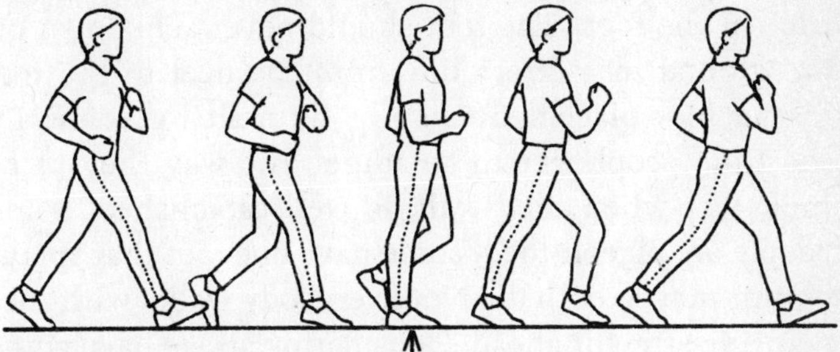

must be straight in the vertical upright position." The illustration shows the point at which both feet touch the ground and shows the momentary straight-leg position.

If the leg isn't brought to the straight-leg position for just an instant, many people look as if they are doing the old Groucho Marx creep. When that happens, posture usually goes out the window and it is impossible to get a good, rhythmic hip swivel and leg swing. One word of caution, however. When you straighten your supporting leg, don't do it with such force that you strain the muscles and ligaments in the back of the knee. The leg should merely be straightened momentarily, not bent backward. If you get any soreness behind the knee, it could be caused by straightening the leg too aggressively.

Proper placement of the lead foot is most important. As the heel is placed on the ground, the toes should be up at a slight angle to the ground. The foot should come down on the ground and roll through from the heel to the toe, with a slight emphasis on the outside edge of the foot. The foot should never slap down on the ground in a direct line from the heel to the toe. Proper foot placement may be difficult for some. By the time people get to be adults, the way they place their feet when they walk is well established. Some people are pigeon-toed; some have one foot that splays out, or maybe both do. Not everybody walks with toes pointing straight ahead. Considering all we have going on with the hips, legs, and arms, I hesitate to suggest that you correct a walking defect while you are trying to absorb all of the other changes. Orthopedically, it may not be possible anyway.

I can only point out that your ability to achieve the 12-minute-mile pace may be somewhat impeded if you can't have a smooth, continuous roll forward on the foot from the heel to the toe along the outside edge. Carol has a right foot that has a tendency to splay out, yet she has adjusted to walk a sub-12-minute mile and has done our five-mile course, which has quite a few hills, in 55 minutes. You just may have to work a little harder to compensate for a foot placement deficiency.

Along with feet that don't track straight, many people have legs that aren't straight. The two most common faults are either bowed legs or knock-knees. I happen to be somewhat bowlegged. Any of the leg or foot deficiencies can affect your ability to swing your leg forward and get a perfect, vertical-line foot placement. But don't let it disturb your effort. Only world-class walkers need to get a true on-line foot placement. If you can walk a line about three inches wide in which

part of each footstep overlaps the other footstep, you are biomechanically correct enough to walk aerobically.

Notice how the inside half of each foot lands on the line in the illustration. The inside half of the back foot overlaps the line of travel of the inside half of the front foot.

Leonard Jansen advises that in addition to increasing stride length, an equally important reason for planting the feet as near to a straight line as possible and swiveling the hips is to lessen the pull on the groin muscles as you pick up speed. If you walk in the normal parallel foot placement method, with your hips squared to your line of travel, at the 12-minute-mile pace or faster, you tend to place an abnormal strain in the groin area. Jansen told me that Bernd Kannenberg, the West German who won the 50K racewalking gold medal at the 1972 Munich Olympic games, walked basically with a normal parallel foot placement. He was such a bull of a man he could power his way along mile after mile at great speeds. Kannenberg finally paid the price with a groin injury that required an operation. It shortened his brilliant racewalking career.

I can personally testify to the importance of proper foot alignment and hip swivel. One day in the late spring of 1985, I was feeling pretty frisky and thought I would see how fast I could cover three miles over some rolling hills on my walking course. I did it in 28 minutes, but didn't realize until the last hill that I had

had a mental lapse and was powering my way along with almost-parallel foot placements. That night I had a groin ache from my earlobes to my ankles. It was tender for a week. All of racewalking's biomechanical movements have been and still are being thoroughly studied. There is a definite rationale behind each part of the racewalking technique that produces maximum speed in a fluid rhythmic action. There are no shortcuts. Even though you may only want to walk to get fit and lose weight, it is necessary to learn how the racewalkers do it so you can get to the 12-minute-mile pace or faster without any injury or discomfort other than a few aching sedentary muscles.

There is a common opinion that tall people can walk faster than short people because they naturally have a longer stride. That has not been proved to be the case with world-class walkers. Ernesto Canto and Raul Gonzalez, the Mexican 20K and 50K racewalking gold medalists at the 1984 Los Angeles Olympic games, are under five feet ten inches, as is our own Larry Young. A study by Dr. Charles Dillman, head of the biomechanics lab at USOC, states, "Body size as indicated by leg length had no relationship to speed." Dr. Dillman further explains, "Stride rate tends to be inversely related to leg length. Taller individuals tend to have slower stride frequencies."

We are back to the axiom that a long pendulum swings slower than a short pendulum. The legs in a walking mode function as pendulums. What a tall person gains in extra distance per stride may be negated by the frequency of strides a shorter person can take.

There is a point where each advantage tends to cancel the other out and sheer athletic ability of the individuals prevails. What is important for you to understand is that a fit five-foot-four-inch woman can walk a 12-minute-per-mile pace or faster as well as a six-foot-four-inch man. Her shorter legs, like shorter pendulums, can swing faster than the longer legs of a taller man. She will just have to take steps with greater frequency. For aerobic walking, it all boils down to the individual's condition, rhythm, and technique.

STRAIGHT-LEG PULL VS. BENT-LEG PUSH

There is some controversy among racewalking experts as to whether the best technique is for the lead leg to *pull* you forward or the back foot to *push* you forward for the main locomotion force. The first style means that the lead leg must be fully extended and straight as the heel is placed on the ground with the toes slightly angled up from the ground. The leg remains straight as the foot rolls forward from heel to toe and as it becomes weight bearing, when your body passes over it. From heel placement until the leg passes under you, you effect a pulling action with it. The second style involves the front leg's being in a slightly bent normal position as the heel is placed on the ground. As that leg passes under you and becomes weight bearing, it is straightened for a moment. When it becomes the trailing leg and the heel of the foot is up off the ground, you push off with your toes, getting forward thrust powered by the foot and calf muscles. Actually, you can walk effectively both ways. Our Larry Young walked primarily with a straight-leg pulling technique (we'll use SL to refer to that). In recent years, however, the Russians, East Germans, and others have adopted the bent-leg technique (we'll use BL for that).

There is a specific reason why you should be aware of the differences between the BL and SL techniques. As you continue to increase your speed and distance, somewhere along the line your shin muscles will start barking at you, and they'll feel like they want to fly off the front of your legs. That discomfort is nothing more than shin-muscle fatigue. It took me a month to overcome it, but now I can easily walk ten miles in less than two hours with absolutely no discomfort. Shin-muscle fatigue for racewalkers was part of a major study conducted by the Russians at their State Institute of Physical Culture. The study is titled "Two Styles of Racewalking: Which One Is Better?" The Russians address the BL-versus-SL controversy and conclude, "We have outlined the basic differences between the two methods of racewalking, and we give more preference to the one with the bent leg." In its assessment as to whether the velocity of the individual is stronger when being "pulled" by the front leg or "pushed" by the back foot, the Russian study states, "The main element, which has to do with the increase of the body velocity, appears to be the foot and the main joint, the ankle joint with its contractors (the soleus and the calf muscles)." (My medical dictionary says, "The soleus is a broad flat muscle in the calf of the leg that flexes the foot, so that the toes point downward.")

Leonard Jansen at USOC, who kindly supplied me with the translation of the Russian study, concurs with the Russians that the pushing action of the rear foot is "the main driving element of racewalking." Jansen points out that the BL technique permits the walkers to put their lead leg down in a more natural manner. This greatly reduces the possibility of over-hyperextending the knee. He advises that women should be especially careful not to strain the muscles and tendons behind the knee if they use the SL technique.

With specific reference to fatigue in the shin muscle, the Russian study goes into some detail that will help everyone understand why shin muscles take a while to get in condition. The Russians observe, "In the BL method, in which the shin is put at a wider angle to the pivotal surface, the foot gets to rest flatly on the sole almost immediately." In the SL technique, "The momentum of forces in the ankle joints is directed onto the contraction of the foot, that is, the tension of the calf muscle exceeds the tension of the shin-bone muscle. These facts are very interesting, above all, with regards to the fatiguing of the shin-bone muscle. It is known that the latter becomes tense during the rocking of the foot on the ground as well as during the stepping forward, when the sportsman draws his toe up" (which is required more at heel plant in the SL technique). The study observes, "In result, the muscle gets fatigued to such an extent that, as often as not, the sportsman has to slow down. It appears that with the leg bent, the functioning of the shin-bone muscle reduces drastically." The Russian translation is a bit cumbersome, but you get the point.

Perhaps this is telling you more than you really want to know, but many people struggle until they can get the shin muscle toughened up. I wanted you to realize that it is a universal problem and is not unique to you. The Russian study clearly shows that the foot action of the BL technique is easier on the shin muscles. Even so, you will have to get them in condition. To prove to yourself why they fatigue so easily, sit in a chair with your foot up as if you were going to do the shin-muscle exercise. Instead, just bend your foot back toward your shin as far as it will come; then bend it straight down away from your shin as fast as you can, as far as you can. Repeat this rapidly eight or ten times and you will start to feel the shin fatigue. This is similar to what your foot does when you are walking rapidly. At that time, you are also supporting your entire body weight. You can see why the shin muscles tire initially until they get in condition.

The best way to get your shin muscles in shape is to walk as far as you can until they are noticeably tired, then slow down enough for the muscles to feel comfortable again. Continue to walk a few yards while they feel comfortable and then crank up your speed and tire the shin muscles again. Exercise physiologists call this "progression and overload." Each time, you ask the muscle to work a little harder and a little longer. It is unlikely you will experience any shin discomfort until you pick up your speed. It was aching shins that kept me from breaking beyond the 12-minute-mile pace for almost a month. Happily, it has not been a problem since then, even when I occasionally walk as fast as a 9-minute-mile pace. I doubt that I can walk any faster than that, so it doesn't present an ongoing problem. For aerobic conditioning and weight loss, it is not even necessary to walk that fast. I do it now and then just to test my walking speed.

On a good day, when you have mastered the race-walking technique and have developed a good fluid rhythm, you may feel like an eighteen-year-old with a new sports car. You just "want to see what it can do." After you get in condition, go for it once in a while when the spirit moves you. It will give you a great sense of satisfaction to know you aren't over the hill.

You now have all the information you need to walk aerobically. As a word of caution: Don't let anybody talk you into carrying weights to increase the aerobic effect. The July 1985 issue of *The Runner* magazine had an article on "The Hand Weights Debate." There is some controversy even in the running camp as to whether carrying hand weights is good or bad. It seems, however, that the "experts" want to weight the walkers down. A professor of exercise science at a major university says in the article, "The main advantage of the weights is for the individual who has orthopedic problems and can't run. Carrying weights, he or she can walk slowly but still raise the heart rate enough to get a cardiovascular benefit." This is wrong,

wrong, wrong! Aerobic walking should be rhythmic, fluid, and *unencumbered.* Don't let anyone talk you into carrying weights.

To improve your walking style and speed you should experiment with the SL and BL techniques to find which one is more effective and comfortable for you. Remember, we aren't going to race; we just want to be able to hit the 12-minute-per-mile pace. I flatly predict, however, that of those who stay with it and get in shape, at least 90 percent will want to see how fast they can walk *below* the 12-minute-per-mile speed. It is a natural curiosity we all seem to have, to find out what our athletic capacity is.

You will find that when you are absolutely sure you can't go faster than a 12-minute mile, if you'll keep banging away at it, you will eventually break through to an 11½-minute mile and later an 11-minute mile and so on. A major reason for this is that increased sustainable speed comes from developing a smooth, fluid rhythm, utilizing your total body. This takes practice and lots of it. It is not brute force or sheer athletic ability that determines how fast you can walk. This is another reason why aerobic walking is an absolute natural for women. As I mentioned earlier, Carol walked me right into the ground until I could develop the proper rhythm to keep up.

I find the BL technique works best for me on flat ground and going downhill. For going uphill, the SL method gives me the best consistent speed. If you use the BL technique, you must remember to straighten the leg for an instant as it passes under you. Otherwise, you will continue with the legs bent. This is called "creeping" and gives you the Groucho Marx look.

One common complaint many joggers and runners have is that those exercises are boring. There's nothing to occupy your mind. Exercise equipment is also terminally boring. With aerobic walking, however, you are involved in a rhythmic learning experience in addition to a conditioning exercise. The biomechanical adjustments to your arm swing, hip swivel, foot placement, and leg action all require concentration, coordination, and practice. You don't have time to be bored. Aerobic walking gives you a sense of accomplishment. It's like learning a new dance. Even though early on you may struggle, trying to get that ground-eating, fluid, rhythmic action, it will all come together if you stay with it. For everyone overweight and out of shape, it is the single best health-rewarding exercise. Other exercises may supplement it, but none are better.

When you master three miles in 36 minutes, you will be fit and well on your way to the weight you desire and the twenty-year-old physique you once had. By that time, you are irrevocably hooked. You know aerobic walking is working, and the thought of going back to your old self creates a sense of panic. The beauty of it is that you will actually like what you are doing. You will look forward to it every day. Weather permitting, Carol and I walk five miles a day, six or seven days a week. It takes some pretty tough weather to stop us. We do it in 60 minutes or less, depending on how frisky we feel—never slower than 60 minutes, though. When traveling, we always try to work a walk into our schedule, even if its only two or three miles. That never seems enough anymore.

Once you get in shape and master aerobic walking, you should do three miles in 36 minutes a minimum of four or five days a week. Beyond that, do what your system needs to stay fit and hold your weight where you want it. You can always do more, but you cheat yourself if you do less. I'll bet you money, marbles, or chalk, that you will feel guilty on the days you don't walk, because you will feel as if you are cheating your body and yourself out of something that is good and healthful. And you are!

To safely get the most out of your daily aerobic walk you should allow a few extra minutes for a warm-up and cool-down walk. Start by walking very briskly with your arms fully extended for about a quarter of a mile. This will help to warm up your leg muscles and elevate your heart rate. Then from the starting point on your measured walking course, check the time on your watch, pull your arms up to 90 degrees, and take off. At the end of a known distance (three miles or however far you are walking that day), check the time and *quickly* take your pulse. You must know how far and how fast you walked each day and if you had your heart in your aerobic training range. To cool down, simply drop your arms to the normal position and stroll in a leisurely fashion for about another quarter of a mile.

This chapter has covered what you must do to walk aerobically and benefit from the perfect exercise. Since it involved a considerable number of biomechanical changes from normal walking, here is a checklist summary:

1. Stretching. Do stretch exercises before and after each walk. Stretch also on days you don't walk. This will reduce some soreness, help your stride, and help your normal walking.
2. Posture. *Very important*—chin up—head level—shoulders relaxed—hips in line under shoulders—spine straight—body erect.
3. Arms. Bent 90 degrees at elbow—hold angle constant—arms swing in sync with leg stride—forward swing ends with wrist at centerline of rib cage, hand no higher than opposite breast—backswing ends with wrist at hip, elbow close to body but not touching. *Complete movement of the arms through the full stroke from front to back and back to front is extremely important.* Don't do it in a namby-pamby manner.
4. Hands. Hold in straight line from wrist—form lightly closed fists—do not let them hang loose and flap.
5. Foot placement. Ideally, feet should track a straight line (i.e., toe of back foot in line with heel of front foot)—acceptable alternative: inside half of back foot overlaps track line of inside half of front foot. If it is orthopedically impossible for you to achieve the foot placement, you should still be able to do a 12-minute mile or better with normal parallel

strides. Just be alert for possible tenderness in the groin area. Back off a few days if pain occurs.

6. Hip movement. Hip swivels forward with lead leg to help straight-line foot placement for longer stride and to lessen strain on groin muscles. Hip drops slightly with lead leg as that leg passes under the body. Hips swivel back and forth with each leg swing. There should be *no side-to-side wiggle.*
7. Straight-leg technique. Lead leg is straight and fully extended as the heel is placed on the ground with the toes pointing up at a comfortable angle. Leg pulls you through the stride and remains straight as it passes under the body and becomes weight bearing.
8. Bent-leg technique. Lead leg is bent in a more natural position as the heel is placed on the ground. As it passes under your body and becomes weight bearing, it is straightened for a moment. The walker is pushed forward as the back foot toes off and becomes the driving force.
9. Front foot action. In both SL and BL techniques, as the heel is placed on the ground the foot rolls forward to the toe with a slight emphasis to the outside edge of the foot. Avoid slapping the foot straight down heel to toe.
10. Shoulders. Shoulders are squared to the line of travel and hang relaxed. Do not rotate or swing shoulders with arm swing.

11. Frankenstein. Avoid hunching your shoulders up as you try to walk faster. It ruins your posture and total rhythm. Keep the shoulders down in a natural position.
12. Groucho Marx. Avoid the Groucho Marx creep by bringing your weight-bearing leg to a momentary straight position.
13. Putting it all together. In order of importance, concentrate on posture, technique, rhythm, and speed. When all of the foregoing become one rhythmic, synchronized, fluid move; when you are totally relaxed and kind of sitting back on your hips with proper posture; when the ground flows by under your feet as you are cruising along hitting on all cylinders —*then* you've got it all together.

Per minute, or per hour, there is no single, always-accessible, injury-free exercise you can invest your time in that even comes close to aerobic walking. It has it all, and it's free.

5. It Looks Herky-Jerky, Specificity, and William "The Refrigerator" Perry

There is a predictable stumbling block you will probably encounter in launching and staying with a lifetime aerobic walking program. It is a self-conscious image of a changed walking style. Until you get used to it, the new gait feels and looks awkward. This causes a great number of people to be self-conscious initially. The altered walking style of the aerobic walker or racewalker is so controversial in this country (and, I emphasize, only in *this* country) that it was the subject of a front-page feature story in the February 28, 1986, issue of the *Wall Street Journal.* The article explained racewalking's image problem in the United States, but then went on to point out that racewalking "is respected and state supported in Mexico, Italy, Spain, East Germany, and the Soviet Union." The *Journal* failed to mention that China, with the biggest population of all, is also an avid racewalking nation with government support for racewalking. In 1985, the Chinese women racewalkers were the reigning champions in international competition.

Because the United States is so out of step (no pun intended) with the rest of the planet on the merits and appearance of aerobic walking or racewalking, a full-blown discussion of this problem is in order so that everyone will know what to expect and what to do about it. When I first learned the racewalking technique almost two years ago, I was so delighted with its exercise conditioning effect that it never occurred to me that somebody might think it looked funny. That subject didn't arise until I held a couple of aerobic walking clinics at our YMCA. Quite a few people said they thought walking like that might be "embarrassing." Two women friends of ours asked if they could walk with Carol and me so they wouldn't "feel funny."

I really didn't believe appearance was a severe problem until a couple of months later, when I was driving down a neighborhood street. I saw one of the women to whom I had taught aerobic walking at the YMCA. She was trying to walk at the 12-minute-mile aerobic pace in the conventional manner. Her arms were fully extended and she was swinging them as hard as she could while leaning forward, trying to compensate with her body for the force of the backswing of her arms. She was thrashing her way down the street with horrible form. I got out of the car and asked her why she was trying to walk aerobically that way. She said she'd tried it the way I'd taught her for about a week but her husband thought it looked "silly," and a neighbor friend asked why she was "doing that funny walk." Her husband and the neighbor are more overweight than she is, and neither does any form of exercise. It is tragic to have a conscientious person intimidated out of a perfect exercise. Instead of mocking something they didn't know anything about, they'd have been much wiser to join her and get trim and fit themselves.

There are also instances where a negative image of the walking style is needlessly self-induced. After my highly successful stress test at the Cooper Clinic, Bob Vernon, Cooper's public relations writer, interviewed me about the aerobic walking style for an article that subsequently appeared in the clinic's monthly publication, *Aerobics.* We were in the patient lounge and I was demonstrating the biomechanics of the 90-degree arm swing for him when an older gentleman who was watching could contain himself no longer and interrupted. He said he was a member of the Cooper Clinic and walked five miles every day on the clinic's outdoor mile track. He did it in 67 or 68 minutes, he said, and then, with a big smile, proudly announced that he was *only* eighty-five years old. Remarkable.

This gentleman was about five feet seven inches tall, and there wasn't an ounce of fat on him. His piercing blue eyes just danced with energy. What was hilarious was that he told me the arm movement I was doing "looked silly." Then he showed me how *he* walked, which, of course, he didn't think looked silly. In an effort to get the good speed he had for a man his age (or any age), he was actually doing a modified version of the proper arm swing. Instead of 90 degrees, his arms were bent only slightly, maybe at a 135-degree angle. He swung them in front similar to the 90-degree swing, but he had to lean forward. In so doing, he lost the correct posture in order to compensate for this bastardized version of the proper arm position. In his mind, what he was doing had an acceptable appearance. The mere act of bending the arm a few more degrees, however, "looked silly" to him. Obviously, "silly" is in the eyes of the beholder, and as you can see, it sometimes has no relevance to reality at all.

From time to time, there have been articles in various magazines and newspapers about walking as a form of exercise. Several times racewalking was mentioned, and it has been referred to as having a "herky-jerky style" or worse. A typical article appeared in the April 1977 *New Times* magazine. In it, racewalking was portrayed as an event "in which several dozen superbly conditioned athletes waddle and flap along like crazed chickens with a severe pituitary malfunction." This lame attempt at humor is indicative of why the United States is so far behind other countries in getting on the walking bandwagon. The author was right on one thing, though. They are, indeed, "superbly conditioned athletes." And they got that way, of course, by walking.

A column that ran in the *Los Angeles Times* under

the heading "EARLY MORNING OUTDOOR ACTIVISTS" described speed walkers as "the stand-up comics of the morning. The human body is a splendid sight in the full lope of a proper run, but the speed walker seems to be pulling our leg, mocking us with his comic-opera motion, and I for one will have nothing to do with him." What that writer doesn't know is that racewalkers can run with the runners but runners can't keep up with the walkers.

This was brought out in an April 27, 1970, story by Hal Higdon in *Sports Illustrated.* He wrote about the complexity of racewalking and the fear of disqualification a racewalker faces if he or she doesn't keep one foot on the ground at all times. Racewalking is a judged event. It is the only sport I know of where the athlete can be eliminated from any placing, even if he or she finishes first, if in the eyes of the judges the athlete violated any of the rules. In his article, Higdon wrote, "An established long-distance runner (who shall remain anonymous) once entered an indoor mile walk in Chicago. Walking with questionable form, he barely broke eight minutes. This failed to place him although he did finish ahead of a woman walker from Detroit." Higdon wrote that two years later in Mexico this same runner was introduced to the woman walker from Detroit, who was a spectator at the Olympics. "Yes, I remember you," she said icily. "You're the one who cheated in that race in Chicago."

Most people think runners are so well conditioned they can enter just about any kind of race. The fact is, *pure* runners (not those who have cross-trained in racewalking) who enter walking races usually get their buns handed to them on a platter. A runner only utilizes God-given speed, but it takes rhythm, coordination, conditioning, and concentration to racewalk. Hal Higdon's story about the well-known runner who had to cheat to beat a woman in a mile walking race is not uncommon. People such as the writer for the *Los Angeles Times* seem to think that runners are top-conditioned athletes and that racewalking is a wimp exercise for the oddballs. That's one of the biggest myths in exercise and sports. In this case, I'll put my money where my mouth is. When this book is published, I'll gladly bet one of the uninformed sportswriters who enjoy ridiculing the racewalking style that a top female racewalker such as Guiliana Salce from Italy or Sue Cook from Australia can beat a top male runner walking two miles in a properly judged race. I don't even care if the runners are Sebastian Coe or Steve Cram, who are world-class champions.

How sure am I? I'll give five-to-one odds—my $1,000 against $200. There's only one stipulation. The runner must be a pure runner and not one who has cross-trained in walking. After all, if running is so superior in fitness conditioning and in increasing aerobic capacity, a champion male runner should have no trouble slowing down to a walk and beating a woman. Bear in mind that male athletes already have a 10 percent speed and endurance advantage over females in track and field events. This would make a natural for one of the TV sports shows, since male versus female athletic contests are uncommon and have a big audience appeal. An event even more interesting would be a 5K biathalon. Walk five kilometers and run five. Male walker versus male runner or female walker versus female runner with no cross-training. I'll bet on the walker every time to win that event, also. I'll even wager $1,000 even money that a female walker could beat a male runner in a 5K biathalon as long as neither athlete cross-trained in both events. Any takers?

In this country, image and glamour often seem to be more important than substance. So it figures that we couldn't be impressed with something as elementary and humble as walking. In other parts of the world, that is not the case.

As the *Wall Street Journal* article on racewalking's image problem pointed out, in Russia, East Germany, Poland, and all the Eastern bloc countries, racewalking is recognized for what it is: a challenging, demanding test of athletic coordination and endurance. Walkers in those countries are universally accepted as top athletes and accorded all the privileges that go with that status. Italy has always had world-class walkers, and currently an Italian woman, Guiliana Salce, holds the world record for the indoor mile. Larry Young, our Olympic medalist, is now in his forties and a brilliant abstract sculptor. He uses the "lost wax" process of casting that he learned at the famous Mariani Foundry in Pietrasanta, Italy. Young told me that in 1977, five years after the Olympics at Munich, when he was studying at the foundry, people from the town would ask for his autograph. And as he trained in the streets of Pietrasanta, the people would shout "Bravo, bravo!" or "Forza, forza! [force, power, strength]."

Leonard Jansen's wife, Debbie, is also a racewalker. In the summer of 1980, she took a vacation tour of France, Holland, Norway, and Sweden. Debbie said the contrast in the way racewalking is viewed in the United States and Europe was striking. In those countries, the racewalking technique was as accepted as jogging is in this country. In Norway and Sweden, it was somewhat of a status symbol to be a racewalker. In 1980, Sweden had some top Olympic contenders. Having spent the bulk of my business career in the automobile industry, I know from experience that we in the United States were the last ones in the world to discover the importance of a quality product. Apparently, we'll also be the last ones in the world to discover a quality exercise.

It serves no purpose to learn an excellent exercise, like aerobic walking, if people are either going to intimidate you or talk you out of it. A great number of people seem to get self-conscious over other people's thoughtless comments. You may need some mental reinforcement on how to handle self-consciousness if it raises its ugly head with you.

Before you allow a carelessly tossed, flip remark to deter you from the rewards of aerobic walking, remember that many things we look at as "normal" today were considered abnormal at first. At the turn of the century, nothing came under more ridicule than the automobile. All the wiseacres said, "It'll never replace the horse and buggy." When someone got stuck in the mud or was having mechanical problems, the standard laugh line was "Hey, buddy, why don't you get a horse?" In today's world, the automobile is now more essential than underwear. "Normal" sometimes just takes a little while to catch on.

In the early sixties, the Beatles arrived from England and took this country by storm. During their first few months here, newspaper columnists, television reporters, and even editorial writers spent more time writing and talking about their "long hair" than about their music. Early Beatle photographs reveal a hairstyle that you can find today on a conservative Boston banker. In fact, by today's "normal" standards, everything about the Beatles, from their music to their appearance, could almost be judged old-fashioned.

We are in a youth-oriented society that seems to think anything done by young people sets the trends for everybody. If the kids (or "yuppies") don't originate it, it isn't acceptable. We have been brainwashed with that nonsense. No wonder most of the people overweight and over forty walk around with shoulders slumped and head down, as I once did. Get your head up and your shoulders back. Bend your arms at the elbow and learn the rhythmic hip swivel and foot placement of aerobic walking. It is the perfect exercise. When the millions of aerobic walkers take to the streets, they will put in place a trend and an exercise that will outlast all other forms of physical fitness.

Furthermore, I'll bet the homestead that it will be picked up and adopted by millions of overweight young people who are interested in a good fitness and weight-control exercise. Aerobic walking has no age, race, or sex barriers. It fits everybody. Someday it will be as normal as the automobile or the Beatles. In the meantime, you're the new kid on the block. Get started and stick with it. If anybody tells you it looks herky-jerky or funny, just keep those arms pumping and your head up and keep walking. Don't bother to respond. As the great Irish wit and playwright George Bernard Shaw once said, "Silence is the most perfect expression of scorn."

Good music is motivational. Exercising to music is the only thing that has kept aerobic calisthenics alive this long, when you consider the exceptionally high injury and dropout rates. Aerobic walking seems almost effortless when done with a portable FM/AM stereo cassette player. One I have found to be very good is the Sony Walkman WM-F15. It sells for about $85 at most discount stores. This unit is compact in size and includes an FM/AM radio with the cassette player. The radio feature is needed if you travel much. It saves you from having to carry a lot of tapes. In the United States, you can get plenty of music everywhere except in the most remote areas. Businessmen and -women who travel in and out of big cities have a wide range of FM stereo music to choose from.

The headset on the WM-F15 has dime-size individual speakers that fit into the opening of the ear channel for an exceptionally good stereo sound—even on a windy day. With aerobic walking, you have no jarring and bouncing like a jogger, so once you put the speakers in place, they are set for your whole walk. I suggest you invest another $15 for rechargeable batteries and a battery charger. A set of two batteries lasts about two hours on a charge. That's two walks for me. Always have an extra set of batteries charged and ready. Even though it's light, the Walkman tends to pull down on your shorts or sweatpants. Find an old leather belt and hook the Walkman on it. Leave the belt and Walkman hooked together and just buckle the belt on the outside of your pants. It saves time, and it's always ready to go, no matter what kind of outfit you have on. I can't stress strongly enough how enjoyable this makes your walk and how it actually helps you develop the rhythm and the fluid action of the walk.

There's an unlimited range of great music to walk by. The Time-Life Big Band Sound series is one of my favorites. I have *Hooked on Classics*, by the Royal Philharmonic Orchestra, which plays Tchaikovsky, Mozart, Mendelssohn, Bach, and others. *Hooked on Swing*, by Larry Elgart, plays Broadway show tunes, blues, Big Band selections, and some of the memorable songs from Fred Astaire movies that really make you move along rhythmically. No matter what your taste in music, you can walk aerobically to it to set your pace.

In case you think I am living only in the past, there are many rock songs and contemporary artists I find outstanding to walk to. One of my favorite contemporary artists is Neil Diamond. His "Cracklin' Rosie" has a beat to it that'll make you move like a hamster with a hotfoot. As a vocalist for the over-forty generation, however, nobody tops "old blue eyes." Frank Sinatra was great in the forties and has gotten better with age. When you walk to his "Chicago," "The Lady Is a Tramp," "I Won't Dance," and others, the ground just flows by. But the beauty of aerobic walking is that it can be done to the music of your choice. Classical, rock, Dixieland, golden oldies, and country and western all work fine.

The music helps you with the rhythm of the walk and permits you to lose yourself in nostalgia if you wish. The heady mixture of music and rhythmic movement becomes a welcome opiate that tends to overwhelm your sedentary muscles. You move and groove with a smile on your face. If you are over forty like me, some of your old favorite tunes will take you back mentally to the time when you had the energy level and the physique you lost somewhere along the way. You can let the music bridge the gap while you are getting them back with your aerobic walking. To develop a lifetime exercise and get out of the sedentary rut, most people need all the help they can get. Walking aerobically to music is a natural. Use it.

Once you realize the necessity of long-term exercise and decide to make the time commitment, that time should not be wasted on an exercise that does not give you maximum benefit for every minute invested. One extra benefit that you get from aerobic walking that you don't get from other exercises is its *specificity.* To those not familiar with the nomenclature of exercise physiology, *specificity* sounds just about like what it means. It basically refers to any specific exercise or sport performed in training or workouts to improve your performance in that specific sport. For instance, a runner would hardly get ready for a mile race by playing volleyball. A swimmer is not going to get fit for a hundred-meter freestyle event by running the hurdles. Swimmers swim, runners run, jumpers jump, and chess players play chess if they want to excel in their event. Specificity works mentally as well as physically.

The specificity of walking is what we face every day of our lives from the moment we roll out of bed and our feet touch the floor in the morning until we crawl back into bed at night. Walking, standing, and sitting, with far too much of the latter, comprise our day's normal range of activities. Walking has been our main form of locomotion for millions of years. Why we try to circumvent it with expensive exercise contraptions or other activities (such as swimming and cycling) in order to utilize our major muscle groups for an aerobic fitness exercise is hard to fathom, especially when the largest muscle groups we wish to exercise are in our hips and legs which are most suited to the specificity of aerobic walking.

Every mile we walk aerobically leaves us in better shape to walk normally. Getting your exercise on a rowing machine or by swimming, for instance, will certainly help improve your physical fitness. But when you get off the rowing machine or climb out of the pool, the first thing you will do is *walk*.

The specificity of aerobic walking builds a strong residual effect for our regular walking. It makes us more able to do what we have to do every day from the time we get up until we go to bed. If we find normal walking is not an enervating chore, we will do more of it. This will contribute to our fitness level and help break the deadly grip of our sedentary life-style. If specificity training works in getting ready for a specific sports event, then the specificity of aerobic walking is a natural for getting ready and staying ready for the biggest events of all—today, tomorrow, and the rest of your life.

The exercise physiologists, coaches, and other sundry exercise experts in this country seem to be locked into a running, jogging mentality. There is an unquestioning belief that it is the best way to get in shape, especially for athletes. Prior to the start of each sport's season, most athletes hit the road to jog themselves into condition. The evidence is abundantly clear, however, that our musculoskeletal system is not really suited for prolonged periods of running. In light of this, I question the wisdom of athletes and coaches who continue to use the old dogmatic approach of jogging as a basic fitness exercise to get in shape for their particular sport. In fact, a professional athlete may be shortening his career and earning capacity by training that way.

I'd like to put in a pitch for aerobic walking as the perfect exercise for professional and amateur athletes trying to get in shape for their sport. An athlete who jogs to get in shape for football, baseball, basketball—or any other sport—basically does three things. He elevates the heart rate and sustains it at a training level to increase his aerobic capacity. He utilizes the major muscle groups in the legs (but not the upper body). And he pounds his musculoskeletal system by three and a half times his body weight every step of the way.

If an athlete walked aerobically to get in shape, he would also elevate the heart rate into the training range for increased aerobic capacity. (Remember, my aerobic capacity was greater than the young professional basketball players' and soccer players'.) The athlete would use all the major muscle groups in the hips and legs, even the shin muscle (which gets little activity in jogging), plus major muscle groups in the upper body because a vigorous arm swing is essential to achieve aerobic speeds. This is all accomplished *without any concussion on the musculoskeletal system.* That needless wear and tear could be saved for the game, where a professional athlete makes the big money. All the jogging miles an athlete can convert to aerobic walking to get in shape and stay in shape could possibly add years to his career and extend his earning power. And the franchise that holds his contract gets the longer use of a valuable asset.

Imagine, for instance, how much wear and tear aerobic walking would save the Chicago Bears' football appliance, William "The Refrigerator" Perry. With every step Perry jogs to get in shape for the season, his 300-pound-plus musculoskeletal system hits the ground at three and a half times his weight—*or more than a half ton per step!* At about 1,400 steps per mile, Perry pounds his musculoskeletal system with over 735 tons of force every mile. If he jogs three miles per day, which really isn't much, his system must absorb more than 2,205 tons of shock, primarily in the legs, knees, and hips. Over a four-week period, to achieve minimal fitness for football training camp, Perry has subjected his legs and joints to more than *61,000 tons* of concussion, and he hasn't even put his football pads on yet. Why do bulky football players like "The Refrigerator" jog to get in shape even though that kind of stress is being put on their systems? Because that's the way it has always been done, and nobody has questioned whether it makes sense or not. I question it now.

In fact, I believe that it may be as obsolete as the flat-earth doctrine for many professional athletes to get in shape by jogging. The scientific proof is clearly established that if athletes such as Perry learned the aerobic walking technique and walked at a 12-minute-mile pace or faster, they would be using more energy, more muscles, more oxygen, and would be working harder while eliminating all of jogging's tremendous shock on their legs and knees. Since jogging doesn't contribute to speed, they could save their legs for running wind sprints in practice and playing the game, thus prolonging their careers for the benefit of themselves, their teams, and their fans. It seems to me that linemen, linebackers, and especially athletes who have had knee problems are foolish to jog to get in shape. They should save their legs for their sport and use aerobic walking to establish a basic fitness foundation.

A good example is Dan Marino, whose strength as a quarterback is his deadly accurate arm. He is invaluable to the Miami Dolphins franchise and himself, but is already playing with a knee brace. For Marino to jog to get in shape for the football season is foolhardy. Why subject a weak knee to the pounding and trauma of jogging when he could get a higher degree of basic fitness by aerobic walking? All Marino has to do is to stay in the pocket and throw touchdowns. Anything he can do to save his knees and legs to add years to his career will pay off in millions to himself and the Miami Dolphins franchise.

Here's an even better example of how aerobic walking can help professional athletes in an entirely different sport. I live fifty miles north of Kansas City, the home of Tom Watson, the great golfer. In late 1985, a Kansas City TV station did a story on Watson's going to an aerobics class to stay in shape, which was a truly weak investment of his time and energy. The *specificity* of aerobic walking probably has a better application for a professional golfer than for anyone else.

If golfers such as Watson and Jack Nicklaus got in shape by walking aerobically at an 11- or 12-minute-per-mile pace, the specificity of that conditioning would make the walking they do in their daily eighteen holes of tournament golf absolutely effortless. All of their energy would then be at its peak for each shot and pressure putt. In between tournaments, what exercise could a pro golfer conceivably do better than aerobic walking? There's no injury risk, and from a pure specificity standpoint it is an absolute natural as a way to stay in shape.

The injury-free training application of aerobic walking by professional athletes (and amateur athletes) to get in shape and stay in shape has never been tried, but the possibilities are endless. If ever name athletes discover the career-extending benefits of aerobic walking for basic fitness training, the image of the racewalking technique will immediately achieve universal acceptance and become the in form of exercise, as it should be. *And you can bet there ain't nobody gonna tell "The Refrigerator" he looks herky-jerky.*

6.

SHOES, SOCKS, SHORTS, AND WEATHER

The most important purchase you will have to make to walk aerobically is the right kind of shoes. Unfortunately, that is easier said than done because the market for aerobic walking shoes is yet to be developed. When it does develop, I believe it will ultimately be bigger than the jogging-shoe market for this reason: walking is the right exercise for everyone. Once the market for a properly constructed aerobic walking shoe is established, we will have as many styles to choose from as the joggers do today. For now, running shoes are OK as a starter shoe. But they are really not built correctly for an aerobic walker.

Leonard Jansen points out that there are two main problems with trying to walk aerobically in conventional jogging shoes. One is that the heels are too high, which prevents a quick biomechanical breakover of the foot from the heel to the toe. The other is that the cushiony construction, built in to protect runners, tends to squish laterally and deform. This forces the body sideways and works against going forward. This analysis was brought home to me on one of my visits to USOC headquarters to consult with Jansen. I had reached a point where I could not walk faster than a 10-minute mile. I was in peak condition, but five miles in 50 minutes was absolutely my limit. I was convinced you couldn't throw me out of a tree any faster than that. Bear in mind that there is no reason anyone ever has to walk that fast, but personal challenges come in all sizes and shapes. Doing five miles in less than 50 minutes was mine at the time. (I have never had a desire to race, however.)

Jansen took one of my jogging shoes and squeezed the heel down with his thumb. He explained that this compression on each step causes a fraction of time to be lost and delays your total foot action. Over five miles, it adds up. He showed me a pair of racewalking shoes a friend had sent him from Italy. There was *no* heel. It was almost like a slipper with no more than three eighths of an inch height at the back of the heel. Jansen said that he couldn't find shoes like that in this country. Carol, who is in her twenty-fifth year as a flight attendant with American Airlines, flies to London, Paris, and Frankfurt, Germany. On her next trip to London, she bought me a pair of European racewalking shoes from Adidas. On Jansen's advice, I wore them around the house for several days to stretch my calf muscles and Achilles tendons, because these shoes put my heels right down on the ground. They have no heel lift and absolutely no cushion. On my first time out in the new shoes, I did the five-mile course in 47 minutes, and five days later I did it in 46 minutes. Shoes do make the difference. When I went back to my jogging shoes for my regular five-mile walk at only a 12-minute-per-mile pace, I thought I was walking on three-inch marshmallows. I use the racewalking shoes only for the occasional day I just want to turn it on for fun. However, I do not recommend that anyone buy competition racewalking shoes for his or her daily aerobic walks. Besides lacking good support, they are too light and flimsy. You need more durability and support than they will give you.

Larry Young, in his racewalking prime during the Olympics in the late sixties and early seventies, used an Adidas distance running shoe and cut the heel down himself to get it low enough for proper foot action. Walkers even at his level never had shoe companies fawning over them. By now you can see that it is not only difficult to find out about aerobic walking, but it is even tougher to get the proper shoes in which to walk. Basically, we need a true aerobic walking shoe specially designed to let us move up from a brisk 15-minute mile to an aerobic 12-minute mile or faster with proper biomechanical foot action. There are quite a few exercise walking shoes presently on the market, but the ones I have seen so far are too high in the heel to get good foot action for aerobic speed.

Leonard Jansen said a good aerobic walking shoe should encompass *stability, support,* and *durability,* with a half-inch *maximum* heel height. The heel should also be rolled and tapered. He emphasized that the walker does not need a squishy cushion. In normal walking, the force of the foot at heel plant is only about 1.3 times the body weight. Jansen says studies show that a competitive walker may only have a negligible increase to perhaps 1.7 times the body weight. Stability is what a shoe company should provide to avoid squishy lateral movement and excessive pronation (pronation is generally evidenced by an excessive inward roll of the foot). Durability is needed and has to do with good, tough sole material so the shoes give you some longevity of use. The shoes should also have good arch support. Once aerobic walking takes off as the national exercise, I feel confident there will be some properly designed shoes to choose from.

In the meantime, don't buy shoes to walk in because they supposedly protect you from something that doesn't exist. I recently saw an ad for a walking shoe that was designed "using the latest medical research and footwear technology." The ad boasts, "Step Flex tread design absorbs the tremendous shock of heel strike." There *is* no "tremendous shock of heel strike." In fact, there is no more shock to walking aerobically than there is to walking barefoot from your bedroom to the bathroom.

Walking is man's oldest natural gait, and simply walking faster than normal does not require a special shoe design to protect us from a shock that doesn't exist. Many people walk their whole lives *without* shoes. This was brought out in an article in the February 1986 University of California, Berkeley, *Wellness Letter*, which states, "About one billion people wear no shoes at all. The few surveys of barefoot populations tend to show that they have fewer foot problems than anybody." The article goes on to say, "Ill-fitting shoes, it is thought, cause 80 percent of all foot problems. Besides causing corns, bunions, nail deformities, and other problems, painful shoes can alter your gait and your outlook for the worse." Don't worry about nonexistent heel shock when buying a pair of walking shoes. Just be sure they fit your feet right and the heels aren't too high and squishy.

Good quality athletic socks are a must. Don't try to buy the cheapest socks, as I once did. They can cause you trouble. I couldn't pass up one of those tube-type "one size fits all" sock bargains at six pair for six bucks. In a few days I was getting blisters under my middle toes. It took me several more days to realize that the socks were gathering and rubbing in that area. A top-grade athletic sock that fits smoothly and evenly on your foot is what you need. Once in a while, a shoe or a sock will rub just enough to cause a blister, usually at the heel. It only takes a slight rubbing per step to cause a blister, because you'll be traveling at about 1,400 to 1,800 steps per mile. Get out the Band-Aids and adhesive tape right away to protect the area, wherever it is. I've never let a blister get so far along as to keep me from walking. Keep the toenails trimmed. Foot care is a major consideration. Those feet are your wheels, and you cannot afford to have them rolling along at less than their best.

Clothing depends on weather, and weather depends on where you live and what time of the year it is. Living in the northwest corner of Missouri, I can speak from experience on just about any weather extreme. In July, we can get 105 degrees and 90 percent humidity. January can bring a Canadian cold air mass down through the Dakotas and Nebraska with a windchill of 60 below zero. My advice is not to walk in either of those extremes. Clothing for walking in temperatures up to 90 degrees consists of shorts and a T-shirt for both men and women. In the country, I peel off the T-shirt pretty quick.

When it comes to shorts, once again, the exercise clothing manufacturers have ignored the overweight generation and geared everything for the slender youth market. The average overweight, out-of-shape male has lumps, bumps, and a paunch. Women have the dreaded bulging hips and thighs. Those are the problems we are trying to get rid of. I am convinced that all jogging shorts are made for prepubescent nymphs or jockeys. I have tried on all the name-brand running shorts, and their short-rise waistlines hit about halfway between the top of the pubic hair and the belly button. The draft around the buns makes you feel like you're mooning whoever is behind you. And I am a trim six feet two inches, 180 pounds. Women's shorts are just as ridiculous. Forget trying to buy regular jogging-type exercise shorts for walking. If you're overweight, even by only a few pounds, they'll test your modesty.

My best walking shorts are actually a pair of tennis shorts that have just a little leg in them and are made of a stretch material. An overweight, out-of-shape man or woman will feel more relaxed in a pair of shorts that comfortably covers all the private parts. Be sure to get shorts made out of a washable knit or stretch material. You need freedom of movement for the hip swivel and leg stride. A light cap or hat for the male with thinning or no hair on top is good insurance against sunburn. Wear sunglasses if you need them. The idea is to be safe and comfortable. Most of the exercise ads show young girls or boys with athletic sweatbands on their heads. I wear one now and then, but when they get soaked sweat runs right down my face anyway. The best way to handle sweat is to tuck the end of a small terry cloth hand towel into the back or side of your shorts. Let the rest hang out. When you get sweaty, you can pull it out and wipe off your face, neck, and arms without ever breaking stride. Tuck it back in and use it as often as you need it. The little towel covers more territory than a sweatband does.

Hot-weather walking can be treacherous, especially for an older out-of-shape person. Don't go out in the midday hours. When it gets to 90 degrees and above, it can be dangerous. Don't worry about aerobic speed, and shorten your walk if you feel light-headed or dizzy. When we have those Missouri July-August heat waves, I generally walk at 6:00 A.M. Even then, the combination of heat and humidity makes it difficult to breathe easily. You'll find that this kind of weather makes your legs seem heavy and hard to move; it will test your resolve. As long as you protect yourself against sunstroke and dehydration, there is no reason not to walk. You don't have to push as hard or walk as far, but don't give up the walking routine. You may not get it started again. Once in a while in hot weather, I start out slow (15-minute-mile pace) and figure to just poke along. By the second or third mile, wringing wet with sweat, something just seems to "break loose," and I finish as strong as if it were a cool day. This is exactly what Dr. Sheehan meant when he said your body will tell you when to go fast and when to coast. Don't assume that you have to hit top speed every day in hot weather, but don't assume also that you *can't* hit top speed on a hot day. Listen to your body.

Drink plenty of water before you go out and plenty when you come back. There's no need to waste your money on some of that stuff that's supposed to work better than water. This old world evolved and brought forth all forms of animal life, including us, for millions of years with just water. It hasn't been proved that the recent man-made concoctions are any better than Mother Nature's original thirst quencher. As we get older, most of us don't drink enough water. Doctors recommend six to eight glasses a day. If you walk aerobically for thirty minutes to an hour each day in hot weather, be sure you drink that much. You'll need it.

Cold weather is the other weather extreme to be faced in many parts of the country. As people get older, their tolerance for cold seems to diminish. Evidently, that's why the Sunbelt is such a popular retirement area. For those who don't mind cold (Carol and I are in that camp), cold-weather walking can be the most invigorating and enjoyable of all. But you must dress properly for it. The most dangerous aspect of cold weather for a walker is not low temperature but wind. A windchill of 5 degrees or more below zero is something to fear. Even proper clothing can't produce a comfort level so you can walk with smooth biomechanical movements. Leg muscles take forever to warm up, and on some days they never do.

The most important rule to remember is to *always start your walk headed into the wind.* It is uncomfortable, but you will find out right away whether or not it is too cold to walk at all. You won't walk far before you'll know if this is a day when you should just pack it in and go back home. If you start out with your back to the wind, you can get a couple of miles from home before you realize that the trip back facing the wind is unbearable. By then, you're in trouble. Frostbite can occur quickly. The other negative to wind, particularly gusty wind, is the natural tendency to lean into it. This throws your erect posture off, and you'll tire your back and shoulder muscles. Even on days when the windchill is not a factor, wind can louse up your walk because it affects your posture. Cold-weather walking without wind, however, is an absolute delight.

One of my most memorable walks was on a crystal clear, sunny, calm day, right after a light snow. The temperature was an even 10 degrees Fahrenheit. Walking down a lonely, quiet country road on a day like that is close to a religious experience. I was in God's big outdoor cathedral. The brilliant blue sky sitting on the snowy white rise in the road up ahead gave me the heady fantasy that I would be the first person to touch the horizon. The snow crunching under each step was nature's metronome marking the tempo of my walk. Insatiable lungs gulped the pure fresh air and breathing came easily. I was at my rhythmic best in a fluid, coordinated stride. I wasn't even thinking about walking. It was just happening. Somewhere about the fourth mile, the total experience so overwhelmed me that I just blurted out, "Thank you, God." I think anything more than that would have been maudlin. Besides, I believe that God appreciates a little brevity and spontaneity once in a while.

Even at 10 degrees, I was soaked with sweat as I pulled up after five miles. It was one of those infrequent times in life when a physical, emotional, and spiritual experience come together and you want to live forever, if it could all be like that. That's the kind of day you tuck away in the corner of your mind to bring out now and then when things aren't going just right. I purposely shared this special moment with you because as we get older there is a tendency to hunker down inside the house or apartment and look out at the world as if we're too old to be active and the best part of life is over. Nonsense! The brightest and happiest people we know are the most active. A walk on a crisp, cold day can launder the troubles out of your mind for a fresh look at life. Don't miss the opportunity. It's free!

Cold-weather clothing should be put on in layers. It is better to overdress so you have to peel a layer or two off than it is to be shivering through your entire walk wishing you had worn more. It is impossible to walk erect with the proper posture if you are cold, especially if you are cold through the chest and rib cage. For walking in temperatures below 25 degrees, an absolutely essential piece of clothing is an insulated vest. The L. L. Bean or Eddie Bauer catalogs or stores such as K mart, J. C. Penney, and Sears all carry them. You really don't need an expensive goose-down vest. A good synthetic insulation works fine. The rest of the clothing can be standard-brand thermal long john tops and bottoms, cotton turtleneck shirts, a nylon windbreaker, a cap with ear flaps or a stocking cap, and warm gloves or mittens.

For outer garments, I use sweatpants and sweatshirts that I buy at Walmart's discount store for less than ten bucks apiece. K mart and other discount stores carry them also. Buy a size or two larger than you normally wear. You don't want tight-fitting outer clothes, and the cheaper ones shrink a little. You don't need high-priced exercise clothes to get sweaty in. You pay a dear price for a few stripes down the side and a designer name. The farm dogs, rabbits, squirrels, and white-faced Herefords I see on my daily walks out County-line Road aren't very status conscious. However, if you live on the Upper East Side in New York City, in Beverly Hills, or in some other affluent area, brand names and the finished look seem to matter. Peer pressure dictates what you have to wear. I don't envy you.

Some people have a greater tolerance for cold than others, so you'll have to experiment with how many layers you need at 30, 20, 10, and 0 degrees. Below zero, forget it. Keep your eye on the temperature and windchill. When in doubt, wear more, not less. Stepping out the front door to test the weather is not a good gauge. You will be tempted to think it is not as cold as it really is because you are already warm, and a few seconds outside won't give you a good indication of what to expect. Put your nylon windbreaker *over* your vest. As you heat up, you can peel that off first and tie it around your waist. You are then in a position to open your vest and let air in around your rib cage if you really get hot. Cold weather helps you burn more calories. That's an added reason to get outside during cold weather for your walk. It also makes you step right along. The faster you walk, the warmer it keeps you.

For some people, breathing in extremely cold air may be uncomfortable. Carol and I are skiers and have no problem with it. I have read that breathing cold air won't hurt you. I have also read that if you have had heart problems, cold air may not be good for you. Anybody who has had heart problems shouldn't exercise at all without a doctor's guidance. The doctor should be the one to tell a patient whether or not breathing extremely cold air is safe.

I have never had to wear more than one pair of sweat socks because I move out fast on a cold day and my feet stay warm. If you are in the beginning stages of a walking program and you aren't up to the 12-minute-per-mile pace, then you may need two pairs of socks for weather in the teens or below.

A walk when it's snowing is an absolute pleasure. Once there are several inches on the ground and the snow starts to get packed, slow down and be careful.

Packed snow and ice are treacherous. Pick your way along and forget speed. If you have to walk on city sidewalks that are icy, either walk in the street (if it is safe) or wait until the walking surface is cleared. If you walk in the street or on a country road, as I do, *always walk facing the traffic.* As the days get shorter in the winter, you should wear some reflector tape on your shoes and hat. Athletic equipment stores have all kinds of reflector stuff you can hang on yourself that shines when a car's headlights hit it. When walking on a road or street, be courteous and step far enough out of the way so that an oncoming car does not have to swerve over the centerline to miss you. In the next few years and from then on, there are going to be millions and millions of us walking every day, and we don't want to cause an accident, or worse yet be a participant in one.

Walking in a light rain is another pleasure you shouldn't miss. Gore-Tex jogging suits cost an arm and a leg (about $200, depending on the pinstripes and bells and whistles some companies hang on), but they are worth it. I'll cheapskate around on sweatpants, but Gore-Tex is worth the investment for rainy-weather walking. It's light, it breathes, it's water resistant, and it works. With a little care, an outfit will last a long time. If you can afford it, get one, because it will let you enjoy the pleasure of aerobic walking in the rain and other inclement weather.

Enclosed shopping malls are great for your walking when the weather is too hot or too cold. In some cities where walking in certain neighborhoods is not safe, the shopping mall may be your only alternative. That's another reason some of us prefer to live in rural areas. The shopping mall in my hometown of St. Joseph is typical of many throughout the country that cater to "mall walkers." Ours opens at 6:00 A.M. to let the walkers get an early start. Two and a quarter trips around the perimeter is a mile. Many of the "regulars" do five miles daily. Some walk at a 15-minute-per-mile pace. This wouldn't keep them at an aerobic level if they were really fit, but it's a good workout for many older overweight and out-of-shape folks, and it may be all they can handle.

Most people at our mall say they are walking for their health and to lose weight. One woman said she lost fifty-one pounds by walking. Several people have had heart problems. One sixty-eight-year-old widower said he likes the opportunity to meet people. He says he has made over a hundred new acquaintances. There is a certain camaraderie among the mall walkers, especially the early birds. The stores don't open until 10:00 A.M., but all the hardcore walkers are there well before 8:00 A.M. I never walk at the mall, but would not try to talk anybody out of it. For me, there is no substitute for nature and the outdoors. I don't find that many bad days I can't handle with the proper clothing. One of the main advantages of aerobic walking outdoors is that you take fewer turns on a longer straight course, which permits you to develop a smooth, uninterrupted stride. There are a lot of corners to negotiate in a shopping mall, plus other foot traffic that might slow you down.

Nevertheless, a shopping mall can be a good place for you to start. You will be exposed to others who have found the miracle of walking. You will hear health-improvement stories, weight-loss stories, and sore-muscle stories. All of it will help you get a good firm start. Bear in mind, most of the mall walkers are fighting the same weight and fitness problems you are. You will find it easy to relate to them. It may mean more to you to have twenty or thirty people with problems similar to yours giving you encouragement to walk every day than anything you read in this or any other book. Just don't get hooked up with a bunch of slow walkers and miss out on the total benefits you can get with aerobic walking. Minute for minute, it is the most productive exercise time you can spend. But you have to maintain the speed.

There is no question that aerobic walking, when done consistently, will give you the maximum benefit for the time invested. People in the United States have more leisure time than the citizens of any other nation. There is a common belief by most people in this country, however, that they don't have time for exercise. Isn't it time you stopped using that excuse?

7.

FINDING THE TIME, WHEN WALKING WORKS BEST, AND TOGETHERNESS

We've all heard the old saying "Time is of the essence." When it comes to exercise, many of us seem to believe "Time is of the absence." There's a loud moaning and groaning and gnashing of the teeth from those who swear up and down there just aren't enough hours in the day to work in 45 minutes to an hour for exercise. One nationwide survey on the reasons people gave for not participating in an ongoing exercise program offered the following: "lack of time" (43 percent), "lack of willpower" (16 percent), "just don't feel like it" (12 percent), "medical problems" (9 percent), and "lack of energy" (8 percent). What a sorry list of excuses! Only the 9 percent with medical problems could genuinely be excused. But even then, some medical problems such as adult diabetes brought on by obesity would respond favorably to a proper walking program.

If you are hiding behind some of those transparent excuses, let's examine them to see why you are cheating yourself. Forty-three percent of those responding to the survey said they lack enough time. There are 168 hours in each week. Can you honestly say that out of all those hours you really don't have time to exercise? The question is, how many of the 168 hours are needed to have an effective aerobic walking program? A realistic number to start with is about 5 hours. That would be 1 hour a day five days a week, which includes getting dressed, doing 5 to 7 minutes of stretches, and walking. Bear in mind, you start exercising the minute you go out the door. Of the hour, approximately 45 minutes should be spent walking if you are physically up to it.

A beginner may only be able to walk 10 or 15 minutes a day for a while. Unfortunately, many people are in that sad shape. They won't be able to spend an hour a day. If you find an hour too much to handle in the beginning, you should walk seven days a week if at all possible. Keep asking your body for a little more each day, but don't let your heart rate exceed the 85 percent training range. Over a period of *months*, if you progress properly, you should ultimately be able to dress, do your stretches, crank off three miles in 36 minutes, and have a total aerobic workout in *less* than an hour each day. The only reasons to do more are because you need more weight loss, you just love walking, or you've really gotten the bug and are training to race. The three miles in 36 minutes would have put your pulse into the target training range of 70 to 85 percent and held it there for at least 25 minutes. This would easily reach or exceed the amount Dr. Cooper and others believe is needed for the necessary aerobic benefit.

Where do you get the 5 hours? Start first with giving that time priority over everything else in your life except your job and the proper amount of sleep. The latter varies with individuals, but the older we get, the less sleep we seem to need. Use your imagination in working out a schedule. For most working people, Saturday and Sunday are two days when a couple of hours can be found without too much trouble. Quite a few people extend their walks in time and distance on the weekends. That's OK if you are reasonably fit, but don't double up trying to rush the fitness program. You'll aggravate your sedentary muscles even more and possibly suffer a setback.

Here's my suggestion to help you find 5 hours out of the 168 for your walking program. Friday after work is a good time to finish the week with a hard walk. It flushes out the workweek's frustrations and gets you feeling good for the weekend. On Saturday and Sunday, you should not let any activity have priority over your walk. Monday would be an appropriate off-day, since you've hit it three days in a row. Walk Tuesday and Wednesday. Take Thursday off because you are going to have three consecutive weekend walks coming up. You may prefer other days. You don't need a fixed schedule, so shuffle the walking days around to fit your week's activities. Four days out of seven is an absolute minimum, and you should shoot for five or more if you can handle it. Studies show that two or three days are not enough to give you a measurable benefit. If you approach your walking program as if you're taking castor oil, you'll never get with it. That's when most people rationalize themselves out of exercising by saying "I don't have time." I should know. I used that excuse a jillion times myself before I started jogging.

Here's a tip that's a sure sign you are kidding yourself about lack of time. If a football game on TV or some other TV program or some other form of entertainment is more important than your walk, you're in trouble. It isn't that you don't have the time; you just don't have the *commitment.* There are very few of us, if we are totally honest with ourselves, who can't find 5 hours out of 168 hours to devote to our health. We all generally find time to do the things we really want to do. I was living proof of this. For instance, at work, I would always schedule my favorite job functions and appointments first, saving the hard rocks for late in the day. Very often they got postponed until tomorrow, and tomorrow, and tomorrow. That's just human nature. Do you know anybody who purposely starts each day with the most unpleasant activities?

Starting an exercise program is one of those hard rocks you tend to want to put off until tomorrow with the excuse "I just don't have the time today." Give aerobic walking a chance to work its wonders for you, and you'll be putting off other things, because walking won't be one of life's burdens for you. It will be an enjoyable necessity. It will become a top priority, as it should be. My gut feeling is that many of those in the survey who said they didn't have the time were not as frank as those who just flatly said they "lacked willpower," "didn't feel like it," or "lacked energy." I can readily identify with all three. I was fifty-two years old before I could sustain a regular aerobic exercise.

Self-motivation comes in a variety of forms for a variety of people. Don't be surprised if you finally get it together someday without the proverbial lightning bolt's striking you. I read Jim Fixx's book on running, which got me started. But it didn't keep me going. I hated jogging. It is important for you to think deeply, however, about why you aren't exercising so you don't continue to put it off for some reason that isn't truly valid or doesn't even exist. For some of us, the exercise light comes on sooner or later, but for some others it never does. I am happy my light finally came on, but I take no credit for it. Perhaps if I had known as much about walking as I do now, I would have been motivated sooner. But even that is an iffy premise. What's hard to overcome is that we have lived most of our lives without any great emphasis on a clear-cut need for daily exercise. Only in the last decade has the importance of exercise (especially aerobic exercise) been so firmly established.

There is one socioeconomic group that has a greater

predictability to exercise. Studies show that the people most likely to engage regularly in spontaneous exercise are well-educated, are self-motivated, and have the behavioral skills to plan an exercise program and prepare for relapses. These are generally considered to be the movers and shakers of the business world and society. Are you in this group? If so, why aren't you exercising?

Conversely, a study entitled "Blue-Collar Workers and Physical Activity" by the Ministry of Culture and Recreation of the Canadian government indicated that its subjects were the most difficult to motivate and the least likely to exercise. The study reported that "(1) fewer blue-collar workers participate in exercise than white-collar workers, (2) they also participate less in sports and physical recreation activities, (3) blue-collar workers participate in exercises both less frequently than white-collar workers and at lower intensities, and (4) there are fewer employee fitness programs for blue-collar workers."

Some companies provide fitness programs for their employees, particularly their executives. In the final analysis, however, exercise has to be a personal lifetime commitment, and it is best if the inspiration comes from within the individual. Nobody who is deadly serious about losing weight and getting in shape should wait for a company to provide the means or motivation. What happens if you leave the company or retire? Does exercise stop? It shouldn't. If you are a blue-collar worker you will probably have a tougher time getting started with an exercise program and sticking with it, mainly because, as a class, blue-collar workers just don't do aerobic exercise. You will not have the daily motivational help of fellow workers who are exercising, talking about exercising, and, more important, comparing the beneficial effects of exercising. Daily exposure to that kind of peer pressure and inspiration is a definite help in keeping people motivated to continue. To this degree, the blue-collar worker is at a distinct disadvantage. If you are in this group, you should be aware of it, because implementing an exercise program will require stronger individual determination. Believe in yourself. You can do it. Don't throw in the towel and just get fatter.

A friend once told me, "If you have your health, never worry about anything that can be replaced with money." Too many people get that backward. In their pursuit of money, they place their health last. They take their health for granted and can't be bothered spending any of their precious time or effort on it. Millionaires are buried all the time, and so far, not one has managed to take his money with him. If some had paid as much attention to their health as they did to the bottom line, they could have been around longer to enjoy the good life they worked so hard to acquire. It is well established that good health and proper exercise go hand in hand. Exercise time should be looked at as a capital investment in your health that will produce invaluable long-term yields.

If you are a successful person with good family and friends, every extra healthy day you can tack on to the end of your life is priceless. All the money in the world can't buy that day, but a small investment of time *now* to exercise and get in shape—along with losing weight, avoiding tobacco, and moderating alcohol intake—might help you tack on a lot of healthy days. Most people have Individual Retirement Accounts (IRAs) to help ensure their financial security as they get older. Just figure that the time you spend now on a proper exercise program goes into your "Health IRA" for your older years. My guess is, someday the Health IRA will be more important to you than the one with money in it.

"When is the best time to walk?" is a question that is frequently asked at our YMCA clinics. The two best times are early and late, with a preference for the latter. Some people are morning types, however, and they are ready to go full steam ahead the minute they roll out of bed. If that's your best time of day, you probably would get more out of your walk then. An early-morning aerobic walk and a shower, followed by a good nutritious breakfast, is a powerful way to launch your day if you're the morning type. You'll feel as if you could hunt bears with a willow switch as you head out the front door to face the daily grind.

A lot of people are slow starters in the morning and have to build up momentum. A late-afternoon walk before dinner works best for them. There are other good reasons to walk at this time. A strenuous aerobic walk before dinner delivers multiple benefits. Dr. Cooper says the busiest time of the day at his aerobic clinic is "between the hours of 4:30 and 7:30 P.M." He says, "I've taught many of my keyed-up executives, both men and women, to exercise at the end of the day as a means of 'burning up' the stress physiologically, the way nature meant for it to be handled."

Another big plus for walking at that time of day is that it acts as an appetite suppressant. Many people have the mistaken notion that aerobic exercise increases the appetite. Dr. Cooper advises exercise within two hours of your dinner to get the best appetite suppressant effect. This is borne out by Dr. James Skinner of Arizona State University, who states, "If you exercise very hard before you eat, you will actually eat less because of an increase in body temperature and a change in hormone levels." Dr. Skinner explains: "The centers for the thermoregulatory system, appetite, and sleep lie right next to each other in the brain stem. When you affect one you affect the others. This explains why you get sleepy after you eat a big meal and why, if you increase your body temperature by exercising, you reduce your appetite."

Maybe that is why walking before dinner is especially effective in warm or hot weather. You come in wringing wet with sweat, drink several glasses of water —or iced tea, Perrier, club soda with lime—and by the time you shower and are ready to eat, you simply don't have a big appetite. A salad, a piece of broiled chicken or fish, a vegetable, and some fresh fruit make you feel stuffed. I strongly support Dr. Cooper's advice to exercise just before dinner. If you are fighting to maintain weight control, the late-day timing of your walk can be really helpful.

I know many people in the forty-and-up age range

who count on their martini or Scotch and soda to help them unwind and forget the daily grind. I used to engage in some of that self-deception. In reality, all you get are unwanted calories and a mind-numbing from the alcohol. When that wears off, the anxieties are always still there. One of the toughest challenges is to convince people how effective a good aerobic workout is for flushing out the anxieties, hostilities, and frustrations at the end of the day. When you've had "one of those days," you never feel like exercising. The depression or frustration will make you want to brood, drink your way out of it, or eat too much, as all emotional eaters do. At various times in the past, under the pressure of business and investment decisions, I've done all three of those at the same time.

My generation was taught that it was sophisticated to have a cocktail before dinner to unwind and that exercise was for the young folks. The overwhelming evidence to the contrary means we've been operating with some bad information. Anyone overweight and out of shape who doesn't pick up on the new health information is literally playing with his or her life. Here are five other good reasons why aerobic walking at the end of your day is a smart move. At an important workshop at the prestigious Centers for Disease Control in Atlanta in 1984, a group of distinguished doctors and academicians gathered to present papers for discussion on the subject of physical fitness and exercise. The Atlanta workshop was careful not to overstate the benefits of exercise, but under the heading "What Is Known" listed the following: "(1) Physical activity and exercise appear to alleviate symptoms associated with mild-to-moderate depression. (2) Physical activity and exercise are associated with such mental health benefits as improved self-concept and confidence and social skills. (3) Physical activity and exercise are associated with reduction of symptoms of anxiety and perhaps improved mood. (4) Physical activity and exercise may alter some aspects of the stress response and coronary-prone (Type A) behavior. (5) Physical activity and exercise *might* provide a beneficial adjunct to alcohol and other substance abuse."

In today's frantic, competitive environment, most businessmen and -women would find unwinding at the end of the day a snap if they tried substituting a 45-minute aerobic walk for that before-dinner cocktail. The ponderously slow process of evolution has prepared us biologically for a different form of daily life than we are leading. Our Cro-Magnon physiological systems are not getting physical activity and exercise in sufficient quantities to handle our excess glandular secretions brought on by life's daily pressures or our excess caloric intake. Simply stated, our current lifestyle doesn't work in our Cro-Magnon bodies. A good, strong aerobic walking program at the end of your day, before dinner, will help flush out the day's stresses, anxieties, and hostilities as well as curb your appetite —a genuine quadruple whammy.

Walking in the evening before dinner is also the best way to handle the temptation to start snacking and eating if you usually get home with a ravenous appetite. The emptier your stomach is, the better the walk.

Get your walking gear on right away, do your stretches, drink a big glass of water, and head out on your walking course. You won't have to go a quarter of a mile before your hunger is forgotten. The harder you walk, the quicker you forget it. And as Drs. Cooper and Skinner point out, if you exercise vigorously at the aerobic level, you'll end up with a *suppressed* appetite by the time you get back home. Just as three of a kind beats two pair, it works every time.

A lot of people belong to health clubs that have indoor tracks. Naturally, if you belong to one and you're paying your dues, you figure you should use it. We have an excellent family YMCA facility in St. Joseph, which I belong to, that has an indoor track. Twenty-two times around is a mile. I did two miles there *once* and felt as if I had been there since childhood. Unbelievably boring! If you try to do aerobic walking on an indoor track and find it boring, don't blame the walking, blame the setting. Common sense tells us that the monotony of going round and round on a ring will drive you dippy. That's no excuse to say you tried aerobic walking and it was boring. Get outside and enjoy God's big cathedral. Get a Walkman and play some of your favorite music. You won't be bored.

If you decide to walk in the evening before dinner, be sure to peel off your sweaty clothes and take a hot tub or shower when you get home. In the summer, you may sit awhile with a cool drink to cool down before you do that. In the winter, however, don't sit and let sweaty, damp long johns get clammy and cold against your skin. You'll end up with stiff, achy muscles. Develop a programmed ritual, because this is the best part of the total exercise experience. Few exercise books pay enough attention to the after-exercise pleasure that can linger through the whole evening. Carol likes a tub; I like a shower. On a cold evening, after a strong walk, you feel invigorated. The day's stresses and anxieties are flushed away. Now you can enjoy soaking in a hot tub or letting the water beat down on your shoulders and back in a hot shower. Towel off and rub yourself down briskly. On cold evenings, we usually take some hot consommé or chicken broth in to drink as we tub and shower. Very often we have a baked potato and some chicken or fish in the oven while we are out walking. Throwing a salad together and zapping a fresh vegetable in the microwave for a few minutes is all it takes for us to sit down to a low-fat, delightful dinner. After the tub or shower is a good time to do three to five minutes of stretches, because your muscles are still warm and supple.

During the rest of the evening, from the moment you step out of the tub or shower, you're going to have a warm glow all over your body. It is a real sense of well-being knowing you've got a handle on your life. You're in charge once again, and it feels good. If you've been taking sleeping pills, you can probably toss them into the trash can. You're going to sleep sounder than a Democrat during a Ronald Reagan speech. The 30 minutes to an hour you walked aerobically gets the process going and the good feeling lasts and lasts. There's one caveat, though. If you go out and stroll along at a 20-minute-per-mile pace, you will not get the lasting, invigorating effect (unless you are just starting out, and the slower speed puts your heart in the 70 to 85 percent training range). Once you are fit, you must keep your heart up in the training range to obtain the effects of a true aerobic workout. "You can't fool Mother Nature," as the commercial says. There are no shortcuts.

When referring to the walking program in our family, I use "we" a lot because Carol and I walk together every day that it is possible. Ideally it's in the evening, but if she has to fly to London or Paris, I'll juggle my schedule to walk with her in the morning. Walking together can be a delightful shared intimacy for a couple. There are many old, tired marriages that have literally become arm's-length affairs. In a large number of marriages, both spouses have jobs. Many over-forty couples have a mutual problem of overweight and underfitness, so walking together makes sense. In fact, walking together can be just as important even when one of the spouses doesn't have a weight problem. A significant reason husbands and wives should exercise together was cited in the Atlanta workshop. It states, "Support by a spouse is a consistent influence on adherence to clinical exercise programs and *the spouse's attitude can be more important than the participant's* [my emphasis]." There is no greater evidence of your support than joining in. Weight control is only one reason to exercise aerobically. Very few people in today's sedentary environment get enough strenuous daily exercise, even if they are skinny. Slim husbands or wives should learn to walk aerobically because they still need the exercise and because their partner needs them. If you've got one of those deadly tired old marriages, aerobic walking is a way to breathe new life into it. Here is something you both can and should do, and what's great is that you can do it together. The absence of doing things together may be why the marriage is colder than a bowl of yesterday's oatmeal.

It is extremely important to be supportive of your spouse if he or she wants to make a serious attempt at exercise and proper eating. Join in and give your total encouragement. Don't be a wet blanket, because there's a hidden reward for you. Even though you think you don't need the exercise, it will make you feel better than you have in years—guaranteed!

Support and involvement can come from someone other than a spouse. Not everybody has a spouse. In today's world, not everybody wants one. If you are alone through divorce, death, or by choice, self-motivated exercise is not easy to maintain over an extended period of time. The Canadian Fitness Study addressed this problem in detail. There are exercise activities such as walking, jogging, calisthenics, swimming, and others that can easily be done alone. The Canadian study said, however, "Very few people do these things without strong social support from friends or family. Even when someone joins an organized group, they very seldom do it alone. People join groups with a friend, or an acquaintance. People are also more likely to start a physical activity program if someone else in their family, or among their circle of friends, is already active." There is no question that people need other people to help them get launched and continue in an exercise activity. Walking is such a natural, it should not require a lot of coaxing to get someone to join you.

You probably know a lot of people who are as overweight and out of shape as you are. The problem is so universal you should have no difficulty finding a friend or acquaintance who needs a walking program as badly as you do. You and your friend must remember to keep pushing a little harder and a little farther each day, however. We have a beautiful tree-lined street called Ashland Avenue in St. Joseph that is a favorite for walkers. It's a level one-mile stretch. I observe the people walking there every day. There are couples and singles of either gender. But many are just strolling and visiting. There isn't a serious aerobic walker in the bunch. The difference between their 20-minute-per-mile pace and a 12-minute-per-mile pace is only 8 minutes per mile. But in measurable results, it's the difference between night and day. When you get somebody to walk with you, you must remember that what you both are out there for is *aerobic workout*! Walking and talking are OK as long as you have your pulse in the 70 to 85 percent training range. Chances are, however, that you will find you need your breath and concentration for the walking. You can visit later.

Make the most of your time. Suppose you had $10 to spend at the grocery store. One store has coupons and bargains where you get a $12 grocery value for your $10. Another store offers nothing special, just $10 worth of groceries for $10. It shouldn't take you long to figure out where to buy groceries. Let's assume you are going to plan a walking program of one hour a day, five days a week. How do you get the most benefit for the one hour's time you are going to spend? Strolling along at a 20-minute-per-mile pace will give you some benefit and burn off about 100 calories per mile. But you'll miss the all-important aerobic training effect. Here's what you get in the same one hour if you crank your pace up to 12 minutes per mile (over an appropriate period of time, of course). You get all the aerobic benefits of a jogger and more caloric burnoff. You can also burn a lot more calories than the slower walker in the exact same amount of time. It shouldn't take you long to figure out the best way to spend your exercise hour.

There are two basic reasons why most out-of-shape people don't walk aerobically. First, most didn't know how (at least until now). But the biggest reason is that it takes real effort. I don't want to sound like Knute Rockne or Vince Lombardi, but what did you ever get out of life that you truly valued that didn't require effort? The things we worked the hardest for are the things we value the most. Whatever comes too easily generally isn't worth much. Exercise is the same way.

8. Osteoporosis and Other Special Problems of Women

The struggle with being overweight and out of shape seems to fall disproportionately on women. Nobody said it was fair, but that's the way it turned out. Women's weight problems are compounded by the role nature gave them in the reproduction of the species and the uneven part they are assigned in various cultures throughout the world, including ours. It seems unfair that for a moment of sexual intercourse the woman must endure the discomfort of pregnancy, the pain of childbirth, and the interminable duties of child rearing. The bathing, spitting up, diapering, crying, two o'clock feedings, and all the time-consuming drudgery that go with raising children from the cradle through high school are borne largely by the "moms." I say, with all due respect, that I would not want to be a woman primarily because I do not believe I have the resiliency and patience to handle it.

To help store energy for the rigors of childbirth and nurturing, nature provided women a way to accumulate fat, especially around their hips and thighs. For thousands of years before and after Cro-Magnon woman, the fat was soon dissipated in the daily struggle to feed two mouths. Now, with an overabundance of food and our sedentary life-style, the fat lingers. Some women who have had several children find the fat is virtually impossible to shed. As men and women get older, calorie needs decrease about 2 percent per decade. If our daily calorie intake and activity level stay the same from ages twenty through seventy, the weight is bound to pile up. The woman who is carrying some fat from her earlier, childbearing years seems to be in a no-win situation.

The pressure to be slim in this society is heightened by our TV-dominated life where slender, attractive women (and men) are delivering the news, the weather, and hour after hour of entertainment from talk shows to sitcoms to you name it. Everybody is pretty and has straight teeth and a slim body. That's what we're all supposed to look like. The role of a young woman today is vastly different from the one the over-forty and particularly the over-fifty woman had when she was young. Today a girl marries later, has more career opportunities, is not hurried to have children, and in general has backed off from having large families.

Women of forty or older will remember the scenario of their late teens and early twenties in the decades of the forties, fifties, or sixties. Many married right out of high school. Some went on to college, and quite a few got engaged and married before graduation. Early marriage was expected. Then came the children, the station wagon, the confining mother-housewife duties, and the fat. And here they are today, overweight and out of shape. Where do they go from here? If you've had that private moment of naked self-disgust where you've looked in the mirror at the excess weight and resented what you saw, then you have only one alternative—exercise. You have already tried every diet that has been on the best-seller lists, so you know they don't work for the long term.

Vigorous daily exercise as a way to control weight is fairly new. For years, weight control was considered a matter of diet only. Just in the last decade, when exercise proponents such as Dr. Cooper have shown the importance of aerobic exercise as part of our health and weigh-control equation, have some of the newly enlightened women started to exercise regularly.

For many women their first struggle with fat starts during pregnancy. Most women find that after the baby is born, the struggle continued. Dr. Gino Tutera, director of Women's Health Services at Baptist Hospital in Kansas City, Missouri, and a practicing obstetrician/gynecologist, says that plenty of exercise and a diet low in fats and high in complex carbohydrates are essential to control weight gain during pregnancy and to shed unwanted pounds in the post-pregnancy period. He says, "In addition to weight control, exercise also promotes muscle tone and joint flexibility, which aid in labor and delivery." Dr. Tutera feels that walking is by far the best exercise for pregnant women and warns that concussion-type exercises such as jogging and high-impact aerobics should be avoided. He points out that during pregnancy women produce a hormone called relaxin, which softens cartilaginous tissues. Impact-type exercises could increase the chance of injury to soft tissue in such areas as the knees and hips.

In fact Dr. Tutera, who regularly walks twenty-five to thirty miles a week, feels *all* women should avoid jogging and high-impact aerobics. He says that prolonged concussion-type exercises put additional strain on the ligaments and support structure of the vagina and uterus. This sometimes leads to a condition called utero-vaginal prolapse, which is a downward displacement of those organs from their normal positions. This could require corrective surgery. Dr. Tutera says, "I am concerned about what the cumulative effect of long-term concussion-type aerobic exercises may ultimately have on a broad spectrum of the female population."

Because of frequent injuries from high-impact aerobics, a new exercise routine called low-impact aerobics primarily aimed at women is being promoted by fitness centers. It consists of keeping one foot on the floor while the exerciser lunges about trying to elevate her heart rate. Maximum caloric expenditure and excellent cardiovascular fitness are difficult to achieve with this unnatural, make-work type of exercise. Walking is the most effective, injury-free weight-loss and cardiovascular low-impact exercise. We've been doing it for several million years, and it's a natural.

In earlier chapters, a number of reasons for exercise and losing weight were cited. Self-esteem and appearance were two of them, and for good reason. Many women on either side of their fiftieth year have gone through divorce or have been widowed. They find themselves alone. New companionship does not come easily to an older woman, particularly a fat one. Again the system is weighted against the woman. If you are fifty, an additional twenty-five pounds can make you look sixty.

An older guy who is packing an extra twenty or thirty pounds can easily get a younger, slender girlfriend or a new wife. A woman, however, with an extra twenty-five pounds can rarely get a younger, slender boyfriend or husband. It ain't fair, but you see it happen all the time. Because many of today's older women married early and immediately became mothers and housewives, they remained out of the business mainstream and consequently don't have job skills. For them, being alone is even more frustrating. They feel helpless and worthless. As studies show, exercise will help dissipate stress, anxiety, hostility, and depression. Just as important, exercise will help elevate self-confidence and self-esteem. There are many overweight, out-of-shape women who want and need all of that. If they can achieve the foregoing *and* lose weight, they are on their way to a happier, healthier life, no matter what unfortunate set of circumstances their personal affairs are in.

In some instances, for the overweight, out-of-shape woman, being married is not much better than being alone. He's lost interest, she's lost interest, and the only reason the marriage stays glued together is because it would be too inconvenient and expensive to unravel. There's not much satisfaction and happiness in that. To help turn your life around, it's important that you engage in exercise that will produce the best results for every minute of perspiration and effort you put into it. By now, if I haven't convinced you that aerobic walking is by far the best exercise for that, then maybe this fairly new and important health reason will help you make up your mind.

Osteoporosis, a medical term with great meaning to women, has crept into our language over the past several years. Once again, women get a bum deal. They are the main victims. The excellent health letter *Nutrition Action*, published by the Center for Science in the Public Interest (Washington, D.C.), carried an informative article on osteoporosis in the July/August 1985 issue. Dr. William Peck, professor and cochairman of the Department of Medicine at Washington University in St. Louis and president of the board of trustees for the newly created Chicago-based Osteoporosis Foundation, explained how this calcium deficiency weakens the bones, who is most vulnerable, and what can be done about it. As *Nutrition Action* reported, "One of the sneakiest of the so-called 'silent killer' diseases, osteoporosis afflicts women more often than men, whites more frequently than blacks, and postmenopausal women most of all."

The malady is characterized by gradual loss of bone density or mass. The estimated 15 or 20 million Americans who suffer from this condition may never know it until a weakened bone fractures. About 1.3 million fractures attributable to osteoporosis occur each year among Americans aged forty-five and older. "The spine, hip, or wrist are the most vulnerable," according to Dr. Peck. By the time this book is published, I am sure most women over forty will be familiar with the many aspects of osteoporosis. However, the old saying "An ounce of prevention is better than a pound of cure" was never more appropriate than with this disease.

Dr. Peck says, "We appear to have better strategies for preventing osteoporosis than we do for rebuilding bone." He advises, "There is a considerable body of information to suggest that *weight-bearing exercise* promotes bone health and reduces skeletal losses. It appears that exercise does reduce bone losses, probably by increasing bone formation." The weight-bearing exercises suggested are walking and jogging.

I have clearly shown that walking is superior to jogging, so now with the threat of osteoporosis you have another reason to walk. Swimming, exercycles, and other exercises that aren't weight bearing (because your musculoskeletal system needs to work against gravity) are not effective. From what is known at this point, you do not have to walk aerobically. But if you are up and walking to help prevent osteoporosis, why walk slowly? Why not crank it up to the aerobic level, raise your metabolism, and peel off some of that fat? It only takes the difference of 3 minutes per mile, to go from a brisk 15-minute mile to an aerobic 12-minute mile.

It has not been established exactly how much exercise is needed to help prevent osteoporosis. It probably varies for different women when all aspects of their life-styles are considered. With walking as your exercise, however, it is doubtful you can do too much. It is more likely you will do too little. Obviously, your own doctor should advise you on diet, calcium supplements, and exercise.

The November 1985 issue of the University of California, Berkeley, *Wellness Letter* had an "Osteoporosis Update." It states, "If you are a woman and answer yes to any *two* of the following questions, you may be at risk for developing osteoporosis." The questions are: "(1) Do you smoke? (2) Do you exercise *infrequently*? (3) Are you fair skinned? (4) Are you small boned? (5) Have you ever gone on a lot of diets? (6) Do you regularly have three or more alcoholic drinks? (7) Have you been underweight most of your life?" Probably 90 percent of the women will have to answer yes on *infrequent exercise* and *frequent diets*. Smoking and being fair skinned (or white) will catch a large percentage also. With the threat of osteoporosis, you certainly have another big reason to take charge of your life and start walking. Why not walk aerobically and get *all* the benefits of vigorous exercise?

As mentioned earlier, the image of what women should look like is constantly flashed at us by the beautiful people on TV, in the movies, and in fashion magazines. Don't assume that you can change your shape to look like those women. It can only add to your frustration and may delay achieving good, solid, attainable results. We must realize that all any of us are realistically capable of is to get back to the best shape we had when we were at our fittest and fully matured. For most people, that was their early twenties. Arbitrary guides on insurance charts also may be unrealistic for you to attempt to reach today, especially if you were heavy at your best weight even in your younger years.

Maybe your genes are working against you. If you had fat parents, evidence indicates that you will have a tendency toward fatness. The shape of our bodies cannot be changed; we can only remove the excess fat and reveal what our fit body should look like without it.

Women cannot all be tall and skinny, which seems to be what most of them desire. The glamorous fashion models greatly influence that thinking. They all seem to be poured from the same mold. And they probably are. The human body's shape, male or female, is the composition of three basic body types—endomorph, mesomorph, and ectomorph. If you understand this, it may save you the anxiety and frustration of trying to acquire a shape that is not possible. For your information, the term *morphology* is sometimes used synonymously with *anatomy*, but it is usually used for *comparative anatomy*: the study of differences in form between species.

In 1940, *The Varieties of Human Physique*, by Dr. W. H. Sheldon of Harvard University, was published. In this scholarly work, Dr. Sheldon developed the first really useful method of classifying physiques. His terms *endomorph*, *mesomorph*, and *ectomorph* have passed into our language. Sheldon classified the endomorph as one with a "predominance of soft roundness throughout various regions of the body." This is the chubby one of the three and most likely will always be fighting a weight problem. That's a tough assignment in life and deserves compassion. The mesomorph has a "predominance of muscle, bone, and connective tissue. The mesomorphic physique is normally heavy, hard, and rectangular in outline." For a man, this is the athletic, Tarzan type. The ectomorph has a "relative predominance of linearity and fragility. Relative to his mass, he also has the largest brain and central nervous system." This is a very thin person with hardly any depth or width, thin angular bones, and almost no fat. We all know and envy one of these bean pole types who eats like a horse and never gains a pound. They also make good fashion models.

Dr. Sheldon suggests that *each of us is made up of differing mixtures of these three basic physiques.* Modeling agencies keep picking girls with a preponderance of ectomorphic characteristics, which distorts the conception of how a normal cross section of women think they should look. Your physique was determined at birth. You are what you are. You can't have a better or different body than the one you had at your prime. But that should be your goal.

Of all the excess weight an overweight, out-of-shape woman is carrying, the areas of most concern are the thighs and hips. It seems a lot of women's magazines know that. The magazines frequently try to hype their circulation by featuring enticing articles on their covers about remedies that will help you solve that problem in just a few days or weeks with no effort.

As a case in point, on the cover of the April 1985 issue of *Harper's Bazaar*, the lead story was trumpeted in big type—"CELLULITE-FREE IN TWO WEEKS: THIN THIGHS WITHOUT MOVING A MUSCLE." Just tell women (or men) they can lose weight "without moving a muscle," and you'll have them beating your door down. Or buying your magazines. Among the several remedies touted was the seaweed treatment. This consisted of "dried seaweed mixed with warm water to create a paste that is applied to target areas like a pack. Then 20 minutes under a heat lamp finishes the process." In backward Third World countries, people who practice these kinds of arcane procedures are called witch doctors.

In January 1986, *Harper's Bazaar* trotted out the old cellulite gimmick again and splashed it on the cover with this headline: "NO MORE CELLULITE, THINNER THIGHS, HIPS IN 10 DAYS." The treatment this time: a miraculous cream designed to rid women of "unsightly ripples, and bumps on thighs, buttocks, and hips." I'll spare you the details of this "miraculous cream" except to say that it's more witchcraft. What exactly is "cellulite" besides a magazine circulation booster?

The June 1985 issue of the University of California, Berkeley, *Wellness Letter* hit the cellulite issue head-on. It said in big, bold, black type, "MYTH: REMOVING CELLULITE REQUIRES SPECIAL TREATMENT. FACT: THE WHOLE IDEA OF CELLULITE IS NONSENSE." It further states, "Cellulite (rhymes with parakeet) is a buzzword that won't die. In 1973, a French beauty shop owner published a book announcing a unique kind of fat: Cellulite, claimed the author, was a tenacious blend of fat, water, and bodily wastes that hardens to create those unsightly bumps and ripples along thighs and buttocks."

The article in the *Wellness Letter* quotes a position paper by the Medical Society of the County of New York, which states that "fat is fat" and there is no such thing as cellulite. The *Journal of the American Medical Association* has reported: "There is no medical condition known as cellulite." The University of California, Berkeley, *Wellness Letter* explains: "Proper diet and exercise" is the only way to get rid of fat. "Rubbing, scrubbing, or otherwise drubbing the thighs will do no good," they add. They conclude by saying, "*If you take care of total body fat, the thighs and buttocks will follow along* [my emphasis]."

In November of 1982, Judith Willis, editor of the Food and Drug Administration's *Drug Bulletin*, wrote a special report titled "About Body Wraps, Pills, and

Other Magic Wands for Losing Weight." Her first three sentences are: "Overweight and out of shape? Want to lose pounds without dieting and eliminate inches without exerting any effort? So do millions of Americans who believe that somehow as if by waving a magic wand, they will be thin and firm." Willis goes on to expose a number of weight-reducing gimmicks on the market that are serving to lighten up people's wallets but not their weight. She says emphatically, "Wraps have no effect on fat deposits and will not dissolve fat, even temporarily. Fat is not broken down by perspiration. It is gotten rid of only when fewer calories are consumed than are needed to meet the body's energy requirements."

It seems that we are under a constant barrage of magazine articles and books that promise to miraculously "melt the fat away." Is that even possible? According to the *McGraw-Hill Encyclopedia of Science and Technology*, under the heading "Fat Rendering": "In low-temperature rendering, comminuted fatty tissues are heated to 115–120 degrees to melt the fat." If it requires 115 to 120 degrees to melt small pieces of fat for rendering, how in the world can anyone legitimately promise to melt ours away? Where would it go if it melted? The human body has a raging fever at 105 degrees. At 106 degrees or more, irreversible brain damage or death may occur. The next time you're exposed to the fat-melting pitch, just remember that you'll already be a dead pigeon before yours starts to melt.

Most of us quit believing in Santa Claus, the Easter

Bunny, and the Tooth Fairy by the time we were five or six years old. But a lot of overweight men and women are still looking for the "Thin Fairy" who will make their fat disappear by waving a wand. I have tried to keep personal experience to a minimum in this book and cover only those things that apply to most people most of the time, recognizing that there will always be a few exceptions. What I am about to write I have not discussed with my wife, Carol, and she will not know about it until after this book is published. How it will play at the dinner table I don't know, but what follows should help every woman understand how fat thighs and hips can truly be reduced.

Carol is forty-seven, five feet ten inches tall, and weighs 133 pounds (give or take a couple). Her big blue Irish eyes radiate the unselfish, compassionate sincerity that makes up her personality. She has a flawless fair complexion that becomes a puddle of freckles after just forty minutes in the sun. Above her full lips sets a perfect, pert, Hibernian nose. It is so perfect, in fact, that from time to time on her flights with American Airlines women passengers ask her if she has had it "done" so they could find out who the plastic surgeon was. Her total being can be summed up in one word—*class.* As must be evident by now, I love her dearly.

Unfortunately, Carol suffered the personal agony of fat hips and thighs that afflicts so many women. When God put her together, I think He just came off a coffee break and absentmindedly grabbed an ectomorph upper torso and hooked it up with endomorph hips and legs. To make the situation worse, she had the dreaded saddlebags of fat on each side of her thighs. She is quite tall at five foot ten and has a twenty-two-inch waist. By wearing below-the-knee flared skirts and dark hose, she was able to hide her large hips and unshapely legs quite well.

One day seven years ago, Carol was drying off after a bath and said she wanted to consult a plastic surgeon to see about having the saddlebags removed. She felt that as she got older they would probably get worse. Perhaps that comment more than any got me started on a lifetime aerobic exercise program. I did not want her to suffer through that. We had both tried jogging on two other occasions, but only for a week or so at a time. We were horribly out of shape, and it was unpleasant to do, so we quit. I made her promise to jog with me for six months, and if she did not notice any significant improvements, then she could consult a plastic surgeon.

It took us two months to be able to jog a mile in 12 minutes, which is hardly more than a shuffle. By the fourth month, we were up to three miles in 35 minutes, and by the sixth month we could do four or five miles at an 11-minute-per-mile pace. We would jog five or six days a week. The appearance of her hips, thighs, and calves began to change noticeably after the third month. It took about ten months for *all* signs of the saddlebags and the puckered fat to be totally eliminated. We also started eating smart. We ate low-fat, high–complex carbohydrate meals and retired the frying pan. We drastically reduced everything fatty and totally eliminated anything fried.

I don't know exactly how many inches came off her hips, thighs, and calves, but I can tell you she went from a tight size 12 pants to a size 8. The interesting thing is she lost only about four pounds. All the fat she burned off or burned up was largely replaced by firm, solid muscle. Carol's concentration of fat was below the waist. Her upper body was actually very slender. It stayed the same, however, and the fat-burning process of her body went after the big fat concentrations in her hips and thighs. Carol's fat was unique because of her build. Most overweight, out-of-shape women are uniformly fat in the upper and lower body. They will experience fat loss over their entire body when they combine proper eating with aerobic walking. They will most likely show the greatest loss, however, where the fat is the most concentrated.

Carol's fat loss was accomplished with jogging, but I believe it would have occurred even sooner with aerobic walking. The latter utilizes all of the muscles in the buns, the thighs, and the lower leg, more so than does jogging. For a woman, another big plus with aerobic walking, which requires vigorous pumping of the arms, is that it greatly strengthens the breast-supporting pectoral muscles. It also helps tone the upper arms, which tend to get flabby. Jogging doesn't do that.

Proof of total muscle involvement occurred on a trip Carol flew last year with another female flight attendant who is twelve years younger than she. This woman is a runner who competes in a couple of marathons each year. On their layover, she went with Carol on a ten-mile walk at the 12-minute-mile aerobic level. She was hardly able to keep up and sometimes had to resort to jogging for short distances to give her legs a *rest.* The next morning the marathoner could hardly get out of bed. Her buns hurt, her thighs hurt, her calf and shin muscles ached, and her upper body was sore and tired. Runners can't keep up with walkers. That's why I was not afraid to offer five-to-one odds in Chapter 5 that a champion woman walker could beat a champion male runner in a two-mile walking contest.

Along with total muscular fitness, Carol has a "Superior" cardiorespiratory fitness. On June 3, 1985, when I went to the Cooper Clinic for my fitness test, she also had a fitness test. Carol's time on the stress test was 22 minutes and 54 seconds, which gave her a "Superior" rating for a woman thirty and *younger*—not bad for a forty-seven-year-old woman who engages in no other exercise or athletic activity. Her fitness level and weight control are solely from aerobic walking and eating smart (low-fat, high–complex carbohydrate meals).

Getting started and staying with an exercise such as aerobic walking will be your biggest stumbling block. If you don't give it a consistent, conscientious try for a *minimum* of three months, you will not have a chance to experience the healthful benefits it can give you. What motivates people to start an exercise and stay with it is not well defined, as studies have shown. I can attest to that. An experience Carol and I had may be the reason we are *both* exercising today. Way back six years ago, when we were in the early stages of our third attempt at jogging, we could hardly go half a mile in 7 minutes. We were both miserable. One day, red-faced and puffing after a quarter of a mile, Carol said, "That's it, I quit. This is dumb. Women aren't supposed to jog." As out of breath as I was, I couldn't resist the opportunity to zing her about some of her feminist ideas, which we continually banter back and forth. I gasped, "If I told you women don't jog because they don't have the mental discipline to stick with it and they are all quitters, you would call me a chauvinist. I don't feel any better than you do. I just have the stronger male discipline."

If I had hit her in the buns with a red-hot poker, she couldn't have taken off any faster. She never looked back, and her adrenal glands must have been pumping full throttle. Carol finally gave up that day at three quarters of a mile, which was a quarter of a mile farther than we had ever jogged before. My tongue was hanging out, and I thought I would die before she quit. From then on, we kept jogging until my knee gave out and we converted to walking. Both of us admitted that we didn't like jogging, but she wouldn't quit because of what I'd said, and I didn't *dare* quit because of what I'd said. That's a strange reason to keep exercising, but it kept us going at a time when we both wanted to quit.

If you don't have a spouse to keep you going when

you're tempted to quit, surely you have some friends. Get a group together and set some goals. Take some hip and thigh measurements and weigh in. See who can make the most progress. "Misery loves company," as the old saying goes, and you are bound to have a few flabby muscles that will get a little sore the first month or so, if you push hard enough. Doing exercise with others will let you share your initial aches and pains. But you will be motivated to continue when you also share your progress. Weight Watchers has been around a long time and has good success getting people to stick to a diet program with encouragement and peer pressure. If you belong to Weight Watchers or some other diet program, maybe you can put together a group to walk aerobically with you. Then watch the fat really come off.

As I close this chapter, my greatest fear is that some of you will not exert yourselves enough to walk aerobically. The dramatic results don't show up until you consistently exercise at that pace. At our YMCA clinics, and among some of our friends, I have taught a lot of women, mostly in their late forties and fifties, how to walk aerobically. After more than a year, some of these women still can barely walk a 15-minute mile, simply because they have not extended themselves. Several have pretty good form, with erect posture, head up, and arms bent 90 degrees, but they move with all the deliberate speed of a gourmand taking a few laps around a smorgasbord table. Remember, there's only one way to walk aerobically. You have to walk a mile in at least 12 minutes.

Throughout our evolution, millions of years before Cro-Magnon woman, the female hominid had to have the strength and durability to carry the offspring and forage for enough food to sustain two until the young one was self-sufficient. There were no refrigerators full of milk or jars of baby food. The only life-support system was the mother, and if she died early, so did the offspring. That part of evolution is still with us today in the wild. It is the strength and durability of the female that ensures propagation.

There's no greater example of that than observing a pride of lions. The male "King of the Jungle," with his large mane, commanding presence, and ferocious roar, is actually a pussycat prima donna—all blow and no show. It is the lioness that has to have the speed and agility to bring down the prey to feed herself, the cubs, and the "King." She is the one who fights off the other predators and protects the cubs. Today, throughout the Third World countries, hundreds of millions of women who barely have enough food for their own survival are still able to produce and raise children in spite of the high mortality rate. The female of every species since life began has always had to be hardy, resourceful, and fit. It is no accident that women outlive men.

In the Western industrialized countries, however, and especially in the United States, the rich, fat-sweet diet and sedentary life-style have made many hardy females overweight and out of shape. Even so, the difference between being overweight and out of shape or the lean, hardy female you wish to be, and are capable of being, hinges solely on your personal determination and discipline. Some women have it, and some women don't. How about you? Of course, there is always the other alternative. You can wait for the "Thin Fairy" to come and wave her magic wand.

9. The Unknown Champions and Other Walkers

For you to truly appreciate what is possible with aerobic walking as an exercise, it may be of help for you to know some of the feats of speed and endurance accomplished by those who take walking to its competitive level, racewalking. As stated earlier, the technique used to walk aerobically at a 12-minute mile or faster is no different than that used by world-class racewalkers. As they continue to push their speed up to the 12-minute-per-mile pace, many people wonder how far and how fast other walkers walk. Some who pick up aerobic walking quickly may want more than exercise. They might have the urge to move up to racewalking and compete. It is inspiring to know the levels of speed and/or endurance achieved by other top walkers. Most people have no idea of the phenomenal times that have been recorded in competitive racewalking in this country and around the world.

The racewalking sport in the United States has been relegated to obscurity by sportswriters and television commentators who don't understand its physically demanding gait. Shoe manufacturers, sports clothing companies, and a variety of other sponsors all flock to the runners with big bucks for endorsements. But racewalkers of legendary stature compete in total anonymity for prize money that a runner of just modest ranking would laugh at. This was brought home to me on May 26, 1985, in Denver, Colorado. It was Memorial Day weekend and I had gone to Denver to confer with Leonard Jansen from USOC on research material for this book and to see my first nationally ranked racewalking event. It was a 20K (12.4 miles) walk held in Denver's beautiful Washington Park. National and world-class walkers had come from all over the United States.

The race was to start at eight-thirty, and the weather was at its best. It was one of those picture-perfect Colorado days you might see in a travel brochure. On a day like this, one would expect an all-star lineup of athletes of any kind to draw a big crowd. As the walkers lined up for the starting gun, I counted the spectators—on one hand! There were exactly four people: Carol, myself, and another man and woman. I couldn't believe it. This was a strong field of racewalkers.

Standing at the starting line was Carl Schueler, who had finished sixth in the 1984 Olympics' 50K racewalk. Next to him was Marco Evoniuk, who finished seventh in the 1984 Olympics' 20K racewalk and who holds the American record for this distance. Then came Jim Heiring, who is listed in The Athletics Congress of the USA (TAC) record book for 1984 as holding four American men's records. Also in line was Ron Laird, now in his late forties but a racewalking legend and member of four different Olympic teams dating back twenty-five years to 1960. Tim Lewis, the eventual winner, and holder of the TAC 10K American Junior record, was next to Ray Sharp. At that time Sharp held the men's world indoor mile record for racewalking in the astonishing time of 5 minutes and 46.21 seconds. In February 1987, Tim Lewis set a new record with a spectacular mile walk of 5 minutes 41.12 seconds. Not many athletes except track stars can run that fast flat out! Then there was Tod Scully, thirty-six years old, five feet nine inches tall, and a wiry 125 pounds. Scully was of particular interest to me because he is the racewalking equivalent of Roger Bannister, who achieved sports immortality in 1954 as the first runner to break the 4-minute mile, with a time of 3 minutes 59.4 seconds. The racewalking equivalent to the 4-minute mile was the 6-minute mile. In 1979, twenty-five years after Bannister's historic mile, Tod Scully, at the prestigious Millrose Games at Madison Square Garden in New York City, became the first walker in history at a sanctioned track meet to break the 6-minute barrier. He didn't just sneak under the wire as Bannister did; Scully blazed around the track in a scorching 5 minutes and 55.8 seconds.

Unfortunately, Tod Scully's first did not bring him sports immortality, as it did for Roger Bannister. As the starting gun went off, I wondered how many people would have been on hand if a mile race was being run and Roger Bannister was making an appearance. The *Denver Post* was listed as a participating sponsor of this racewalking event, but there had been no feature story on Scully or the Olympic racewalkers in the paper that morning. But that's par for the course. Racewalking is ignored in every city in this country. What kind of prize money did this all-star lineup of world-class walkers get for their efforts? To win any money at all, they had to have raced the previous day in a 5K event and then in the 20K race on Sunday. Based on total points from the two events, the prize money was distributed as follows: first place, $500; second place, $350; third place, $250; fourth, fifth, and sixth places, $100. All walkers had to pay their own transportation and room and board.

There was also the same prize money distribution for two women's events—a 5K race on Saturday followed by a 10K on Sunday. Maryanne Torrellas, the winner of the 5K, is a superb athlete who holds the TAC American women's record for the mile in the blistering time of 6 minutes and 51.7 seconds. Not many women can *run* that fast. Racewalking is ideally suited for women, and they can racewalk in phenomenal times. The women's world record for the outdoor mile was set by Sue Cook of Australia in 1981 at 6 minutes and 47.09 seconds. The fastest woman walker in the world as of this writing is Giuliana Salce of Italy, who set the indoor world's record in 1984 with an amazing 6 minutes and 43.59 seconds.

Lest you think that running a less-than-4-minute mile, as Bannister did, is more difficult than walking a less-than-6-minute mile, as Scully did, I can only point out that it took twenty-five years longer for any human being in the world to do it. Why we ignore an obviously good, injury-free exercise such as aerobic walking and a demanding athletic event such as racewalking in this country may be for reasons of timing and lack of knowledge. I truly believe that in the coming decade all forms of walking will become the dominant forms of fitness exercise. Racewalking will take on a new and well-deserved stature.

For now, however, a trivia question sure to stump ninety-nine out of a hundred people in this country is: What is the longest Olympic track-and-field event? From previous discussion, you already know it's the 50K (31.1 miles) racewalk. We are so running oriented and marathon saturated, however, that the quick answer from most people will be the marathon.

One of the biggest sports heroes in Mexico is thirty-seven-year-old Raul Gonzalez. On August 11, 1984, Gonzales wiped out the Olympic competition in the 50K racewalk at Los Angeles by setting a new Olympic record of 3 hours 47 minutes and 27 seconds, beating the second-place finisher by 6 minutes. That's walking an average of 7 minutes and 19 seconds per mile for the thirty-one plus miles! This was an astonishing pace and test of endurance over a distance five miles longer than the marathon.

Strictly enforced racewalking rules caused five of the thirty-four starters to be disqualified. A walker can be disqualified for not having continuous foot contact with the ground (both feet cannot be off the ground at one time). If the supporting leg is not momentarily straightened in the vertical position as it passes under the body, this is also a cause for disqualification. Any combination of the two infractions (loss of contact and/or bent knee) resulting in three disqualification cards from the three different judges will result in a walker's being disqualified. The dreaded "DQ" (disqualified) is feared more by every racewalker than defeat.

The marathoners have been lionized, glamorized, and idolized in this country, but in my obviously biased opinion they are not the athletic equals of the 50K racewalkers. Consider this: Marathoners are using a natural gait to their maximum athletic ability and are free to run, walk, jog, or whatever suits their pleasure or condition of stress during the race with no worry of disqualification.

The 50K racewalker, on the other hand, must have the endurance to go five miles farther than a marathoner with total mental and physical discipline each step of the way to comply with the racewalking rules or risk DQ. At those phenomenal speeds, he is constantly fighting the natural instinct to run while trying to keep one foot on the ground. As in cross-country skiing, vigorous arm movement by the racewalker must be coordinated with the leg action to maintain a smooth, fluid, and consistent stride. All of this is done at a walking speed well in excess of most people's ability to run. From your head to your toes, the physical act of racewalking (or aerobic walking) requires more total muscle involvement and coordination than running.

If you show that statement to a runner, he will claim that I'm crazy. If the doubter can run an 8-minute mile, just ask him to try to walk a 10-minute mile. I can now do both, but I'll guarantee you that running an 8-minute mile is a big yawn compared to walking a 10-minute mile. This is why the pace of 7 minutes and 19 seconds per mile that Gonzalez held for over thirty-one miles is a remarkable ironman performance. Keeping every phase of the body in sync over that distance requires enormous concentration, coordination, and endurance. The record-breaking performance of Gonzalez is even more impressive when you consider that it was over a shadeless asphalt course outside the coliseum on Exhibition Boulevard with an intense sun beating down. Radiant heat was estimated at up to 120 degrees. Walkers were dropping like flies. Over a third of the thirty-four starters did not finish, including three walkers who comprised the entire Canadian team.

Another major national hero in Mexico is Ernesto Canto. Eight days before the 50K race, Canto won the gold medal in the 20K racewalk (12.4 miles), also in a new Olympic record time of 1 hour 23 minutes 13 seconds. Canto walked the distance averaging a mile every 6 minutes and 42 seconds. His countryman Raul Gonzalez was breathing down his neck all the way and finished only 7 seconds behind to capture the silver medal.

As mentioned before, one place where racewalking is taken seriously and not subject to ridicule is Russia. This is borne out by the results of a USA-USSR 20 K-Dual Meet that dates back to 1958. This racewalking event has been held eighteen times over that span of years, and the Russians have beaten us seventeen times. Only in 1977 did a U.S. walker, Neal Pyke, manage a victory. In a USA-USSR Junior 10K Dual Meet held annually from 1972 through 1979, the Russians won all eight times. Out of a total of twenty-six head-to-head racewalking encounters with the Russians, they have taken home the bacon twenty-five times. They do indeed take their racewalking seriously in Russia. Another place where racewalking gets serious attention is in China. There the women are the top walkers. Out of the top five 1985 women's world 10K rankings, Chinese women racewalkers are ranked first, second, and fifth. The third and fourth places go to the Russian women. There is a movement under way to include a women's 10K racewalk in some future Olympic competition. You can bet the Chinese and Russians will dominate.

We do not have the caliber of racewalkers, male or female, in this country to be a creditable Olympic threat. Larry Young, our only Olympic medalist at the current distances, told me we would not be a viable racewalking contender until we recognized the sport as a track and field event in our high schools and NCAA colleges. We don't have enough young athletes taking up the sport and being encouraged and coached at those levels. Consequently, we have a very narrow base of walkers to choose from for world-class events. It is ironic that the United States is superior to Russia and China in so many aspects of life, but isn't competitive with them in the oldest form of human locomotion—walking.

Those of you who decide to take charge of your lives and learn aerobic walking may become interested in learning and reading more about racewalking, even if you, like me, have no desire to compete. There is only one publication about racewalking that has stood the test of time. It is the *Ohio Racewalker*, now in its twenty-second year of continuous publication because of the perseverance and dedication of its publisher, Jack Mortland. Mortland, who was a hurdler and anchorman on the mile relay team at Bowling Green University, took up racewalking and made the 20K team at the 1964 Tokyo Olympics. He lives on a shady street in north Columbus, Ohio, and is a technical editor and writer for the internationally famous Battelle Memorial Institute in that city.

On my desk as I write this chapter, I have the May 1985 copy of *Runner's World* that proudly proclaims on the cover: "THE LEADER FOR 19 YEARS—MORE THAN TWO MILLION READERS." In the October 1985 issue of the *Ohio Racewalker*, Jack Mortland released his annual "Statement of Ownership, Management, and Circulation" as required by the U.S. Postal Service. Under line item 10C, "Total Paid Circulation," he lists *458*. As you can see, racewalking is not only held up to unjust ridicule but the hardcore number of racewalkers is indeed very small. In a country that traditionally roots for the underdog, perhaps you might wish to become part of this small family of fitness buffs.

The *Ohio Racewalker*, a little fourteen-page booklet-like publication, is chock-full of racewalking results from all over the United States, plus major races in other parts of the world. Various racewalking clubs throughout the country keep in touch with Mortland about their activities and upcoming races. Discussions about various aspects of the racewalking technique are covered from time to time by coaches and nationally ranked competitors.

If aerobic walking makes you want to try racewalking, or if you were a competitive runner who had to quit because of injuries but who still likes the thrill of competition, you can find out where the action is in the *Ohio Racewalker*. It is published monthly from Jack Mortland's house at 3184 Summit Street, Columbus, Ohio, 43202. Subscriptions are $5 per year ($7 for first-class mail, $11 for overseas airmail).

A sports trivia question sure to stump everybody is: Who was the oldest person ever to win an Olympic athletic medal? The answer is Tebbs Lloyd Johnson, and as you might expect, he was a racewalker. In 1948, he won the bronze medal in the Olympic 50K racewalk at the tender age of forty-eight. Everyone should take heart in that. Walkers don't get older—they just get tougher.

Another question for sports trivia buffs: Who is America's most decorated amateur athlete? If the name Ron Laird isn't familiar, it's because he is a racewalker. He is also officially the most decorated amateur athlete in the United States. The May 1985 *Ohio Racewalker* credits Laird with sixty-five career national titles—the first in 1958, the last in 1976. He was on the 1960, 1964, 1968, and 1976 Olympic teams. An injury in 1972 was probably the only reason he didn't make that team. At one time or another, Laird has set over eighty-one United States records and has been named to sixteen All-American Teams and thirty-one international tours (during two of which he went undefeated in a total of twenty-four races). In 1986, Ron Laird became the first racewalker to be inducted into our National Track and Field Hall of Fame and was finally given the recognition he so richly deserves.

The first American ever to win an Olympic walking medal was Joseph B. Pearman, who brought home the 10K racewalking silver medal in the 1920 Olympic Games at Antwerp, Belgium. The 10K is no longer an Olympic distance. Larry Young is the only other American to win an Olympic racewalking medal.

Another of the great old-time walkers was Daniel O'Leary, who managed to cover 500 miles in six days at the West Side rink at Chicago. That's averaging 83.3 miles per day walking and is a truly remarkable performance. O'Leary bragged: "I am a young man with white hair and I thank the Almighty that I am such, and I say emphatically that there are thousands of tottery, complaining old men who might be just as vigorous and youthful as I am if they did but follow my example of walking steadily every day and living simply."

For all the runners, ex-runners, masochists, and out-of-shape folks who are skeptical about whether walking presents enough of a challenge to fool with, let me introduce you to America's premier test of endurance, the National 100-Mile Walking Championship held in late September or early October at Columbia, Missouri. It is sponsored by the Columbia Track Club and is an athletic event unique in all of the United States.

Those who complete the hundred-mile event conducted under The Athletics Congress racewalking rules in less than twenty-four hours join the most exclusive group of endurance athletes in the United States—the Centurions. So far, since the annual hundred-mile race was revived in 1967, only thirty-nine walkers have become Centurions, including four women. Actually, if we go back to 1878, there are three more Centurions, making the total forty-two in the whole United States over a period of 108 years. In 1976, the *Kansas City Star* did a feature story on the Columbia hundred-miler and the Centurions. The *Star* reported that the first Centurion race was a competitive racewalking event held in New York City in May 1878. The goal in that race was to see how many miles professionals could walk in thirty-six hours and amateurs in twenty-four hours. Fourteen professionals set out at 11:00 A.M., followed by twenty amateurs at 11:00 P.M. Since the professionals were walking for money, they were not included in the list of Centurions. Three amateurs—J. Schmidt, M. J. Ennis, and J. B. Gillie—became America's first official Centurions.

The *New York Times* reported that Ennis had worked a full day at a Harlem foundry. He returned home at 6:00 P.M., washed up, and ate supper. Although he had no training and had never walked in a race before, he went down to the track for the 11:00 P.M. amateur start and walked 103 miles in 23 hours 13 minutes and 56 seconds. J. B. Gillie, according to the *Times*, was a "very tall, very thin young man whose legs resembled two matches stuck in the end of a lead pencil." Nevertheless, he was the top amateur in the hundred-mile race, with a time of 21 hours and 42 seconds. The race was not held again until it was revived by the Columbia Track Club eighty-nine years later in 1967. It has been an annual event through 1985. At the conclusion of the 1985 race, it was decided to hold it every other year because of the small number of entries. It takes thirty people to conduct the race and there were only twenty-three starters each year in 1984 and 1985.

The "100" is a severe test of mental and physical endurance that starts at 1:00 P.M. on Saturday, continues through the night, and concludes twenty-four hours later on Sunday. It is held at Hickman Field, the track and football stadium for Hickman High School in Columbia. One hundred miles is 402.3 laps around the track. Perhaps as this country wakes up to the superb fitness exercise of aerobic walking and the challenging sport of racewalking, the number of Centurions will grow. The average age of the hardiest Centurion walkers may prove that walking is the exercise for the over-forty generation. Of the twenty-three entrants in 1984, for example, more than half the starters were over forty. Twice as many were over fifty as were under thirty. The first one to drop out after 122 laps was a seventeen-year-old boy. The old-timers were still going.

In its first year, 1967, a quiet *sixty-year-old* lumberman from Kalispell, Montana, named Larry O'Neil came to Columbia and walked the "100" in 19 hours 24 minutes and 34 seconds. This was an American outdoor record for the distance that stood for eleven years. O'Neil averaged a mile every 11.6 minutes. They grow them tough in Montana, because O'Neil completed six "100"s. The last was ten years later at the age of seventy, in 21 hours 55 minutes and 23 seconds. That was averaging just over 13 minutes per mile. At seventy, O'Neil slowed down a little, but how many people can walk even one mile at a 13-minute pace, let alone a hundred miles?

In 1971, a cloudburst left three inches of water on the track, and the event was moved to an indoor track. O'Neil's outdoor record would have surely fallen that year if it hadn't rained. Our 50K Olympic medalist, twenty-eight-year-old Larry Young, who was at his prime and preparing for the 1972 Olympics at Munich, entered the race. He set an American indoor record of

18 hours 7 minutes and 12 seconds that still stands. O'Neil's outdoor record remained intact. Young said he had never experienced any physical challenge equal to the "100" in his entire racewalking career. Over such an extended period of time, it requires enormous mental concentration and courage to force burning shins and throbbing muscles to keep moving in spite of the pain.

It is interesting to note that of the thirty-nine Centurions since 1967, more than half, twenty-three of them, were over forty when they qualified for this exclusive club. So far only six people under the age of thirty are Centurions. People come to the "100" from all over the United States, but the number of people who race is small, and the number who finish is even smaller. Only a handful of friends, husbands, wives, sweethearts, and sympathizers come to watch. Why do people compete in this form of self-inflicted physical torture? The answers are pretty much the standard kind you get at any endurance event: "Because I've done everything else," "Just because it's there," and "Thousands of people finish marathons, but only a few finish the '100,' " are some of the typical comments from the hundred-mile participants. Some have won races at various distances against other people and now just want to test themselves against the distance and the clock. As reported in the *Kansas City Star*, such was the case of thirty-seven-year-old Shaul Ladany of Tel Aviv, Israel. In 1973, Ladany, an Israeli reserve officer, happened to be in New York. He had won races at most other distances. He flew out to Columbia and walked the "100" in near record time of 19 hours 38 minutes and 26 seconds. He was just a little more than 13 minutes over Larry O'Neil's record. Ladany became the seventh modern-day Centurion on October 7. He barely finished the race in time to catch a jet for Tel Aviv and the October war.

The most durable of all the Centurions over forty is Leonard Busen of St. Louis, who had beaten the "100" a dozen times. The first woman Centurion was Elsie McGarvey of Kalispell, Montana, at the age of forty-nine in 1978. She repeated two years later at the tender age of fifty-one. They grow men *and* women tough in Kalispell, Montana. "Life begins at forty" certainly seems to apply to the walkers.

The man who finally broke Larry O'Neil's record is Alan Price of Washington, D.C., who did it in 1978 at the age of thirty-one in his very first attempt. Price has won the Columbia hundred-miler every year since, and in 1984 broke his own 1978 record and set a new American outdoor hundred-mile record that still stands at 18 hours 46 minutes and 13 seconds. He's the best hundred-miler in this country by a wide margin. The current official hundred-mile world record is held by Hector Neilson of Britain and was set in Walton, England, on October 14 and 15, 1960, in the impressive time of 17 hours 18 minutes 51 seconds. In an interview with the *Columbia Daily Tribune* after his 1984 record walk, Price told how he first came to Columbia in 1978. He said, "I heard about the race in Columbia in an ad in *Runners' World* along with a feature on one of the guys who won a lot. They had some times in there, and I said, 'I can do this.' So I told everyone in D.C. I was going to Columbia and set a record. I had a hard time getting the money for the trip, but I always knew I would go. I was kind of the dark horse figuratively and literally."

Alan Price was referring to his race by that remark. He is a black in a sport that does not seem to attract blacks. Black racewalkers are about as common as black hockey goalies. He had never walked in a race longer than 50 miles prior to 1978. Price was actually a "closet walker," and he said he felt funny practicing in the daylight, so he would go to the track at Bennicker Junior High in Washington, D.C., after dark and practice in the pitch black. Here's a case where the Russian athletic understanding is clearly ahead of ours. Racewalkers don't have to hide or be subjected to senseless ridicule in Russia. Alan Price is some tough athlete and has reason to be proud of his accomplishments. He told the Columbia reporter, "People who don't do this think it's easy. That's because they haven't tried it yet." Price enjoys telling about entering a 100-mile race in San Diego in 1982 where the promoters wanted a "name athlete" for a big draw. They got Don Choi, who held the American distance record for a six-day run of more than 450 miles. The race promoters figured walking a 100-miler would be a piece of cake for him. Price blew him away in 19 hours 35 minutes and 44 seconds. "Well, he finished it," Price said, "but I'm telling you, he was hurting pretty bad. I asked him which he thought was harder, a six-day run or a hundred-mile walk. He said, 'No doubt about it, a hundred-miler.' " Alan Price liked having the best in another sport invade his turf and come away shaking his head. Alan Price has completed fifteen hundred-milers through 1984, more than any other person in the United States.

In 1984, at the age of thirty-seven, Price, who is only five feet seven inches tall, weighed 138 pounds at the start of his record-setting performance. He weighed 127 pounds at the finish. During the race, he consumed a quarter of a large watermelon, a half gallon of apple juice, and a pint of water. Alan Price has not worked steadily since 1979. There are no fat endorsement contracts from shoe companies and clothing manufacturers for racewalkers; consequently, they have to cut corners wherever possible to save money. Price set his American record wearing a $1.90 pair of discounted Foot Locker shoes he picked out of a pile on a clearance sale table. Such is the humble life of a racewalker in the United States—even a champion.

The Boston Marathon has the tradition; the New York and Chicago marathons have the big money; but the thirty-nine men and women Centurions have exclusivity. It takes a special kind of person to do the "100." For those who think there aren't any serious athletic challenges for the exercise walkers, join the Centurions—if you can. People just starting to walk can go as far and as fast as their determination and discipline will take them. By slowly working yourself into shape and picking up your speed to the aerobic level, you will have mastered the perfect fitness exercise, which you can do the rest of your life. And if the competitive bug bites you, there are races all over the country, and the granddaddy of them all, the hundred-miler, awaits you at Columbia, Missouri.

Jack Mortland estimates there are over a thousand Centurions in England. Other European countries also have larger numbers of people who do the "100." The soft, sedentary over-forty generation and the young people in the United States have yet to discover the ultimate challenge. After you have gotten your twenty-year-old physique and energy level back by eating smart and walking aerobically, you may feel so fit and feisty that competition racewalking or becoming a Centurion is just the challenge you need. The real satisfaction, however, comes from feeling so good that *nothing* seems out of reach. How long has it been since you've felt that way?

10.

A PARTING WORD

I have made no effort to conceal my obvious bias toward aerobic walking as the one exercise superior to all others. The physical benefits for the time invested are remarkable. But I will restate something buried in an earlier chapter that you might have forgotten: If you are doing another exercise or using exercise equipment that truly meets the requirements for sustained aerobic benefit, if it is working, if it is injury free, if you like it and will do it regularly long term, then stay with it. Do whatever works for you—even jogging. You still would be wise to learn aerobic walking. It will increase the pleasure you derive from everyday walking. It will also give you an alternate exercise to switch to in case of injury from your other exercise or for variety to avoid exercise burnout.

Remember, walking and running are the only natural activities we use for exercise. Calisthenics, exercise equipment, and even swimming are unnatural. We are terrestrial beings—land animals. No animal species, human or otherwise, engages in unnatural make-work exercise activity over the long term. If you won't stay with something as injury free and normal as walking, which we've been doing since our earliest known ancestors over four million years ago, what is the likelihood that you will stay with an arbitrarily devised man-made exercise? Not much.

Once you find the exercise groove that fits you, focus your attention on the other half of your weight problem—food. That other half, which I call *eating smart*, requires each of us to completely rethink and rework the composition of his or her daily food intake. Dieting (as in denial) ultimately should be forgotten entirely. It never has worked long term for most people and probably never will. By combining aerobic exercise with the proper food groups such as fruits, grains, vegetables, and low-fat meat and dairy products, you can eat normally and maintain the weight you want.

You will have to do some calorie counting during the initial weight-loss period, but you should only have to cut back about 300 to 500 calories a day. By eating the right foods, you will lose weight easier and be less inclined to gain it back. Over the past several decades, the definition of what foods are "right" has changed quite a bit. Years ago there was no mention of cholesterol, polyunsaturated fats, monosaturated fats, fiber, and all the terms that we see and hear so often today. Protein, as in beef, was big. Not long ago we were advised to eat lots of protein and stay away from starches such as beans, potatoes, bread, and spaghetti. I was a poor kid during the Depression; our family ate lots of beans, potatoes, and spaghetti because that's all we could afford. Only the rich could afford steak. I was a senior in college before I ever ate steak in a restaurant. Lord, it was good!

After World War II and through the fifties, sixties, and early seventies, beef was king in the United States. Steak houses sprouted up everywhere. Every cab driver in every city could tell you where to get "the best steak in town." Being able to go out to a steak house for dinner on Saturday night was what many of us worked a little harder to afford. The cruel irony is that, after working our whole lives and maybe accumulating a modest bit of affluence, we are now told that steak is bad for us and that we should go back to beans, potatoes, and spaghetti. It hardly seems fair. But it isn't all bad. Because of high cholesterol, I have been on a high–complex carbohydrate, low-fat diet for several years, and there's no question that I feel better, have a higher energy level, and can maintain my weight easily. The low-fat, high–complex carbohydrate combination that works to lower cholesterol is equally effective in lowering weight when combined with aerobic exercise.

Nutrition and proper eating are in a state of flux.

Most of what we learned twenty years ago is outdated, and researchers keep moving the goalposts on us. Much of the information is as garbled and confusing as is the exercise advice. You have to be careful of your sources or you might be getting information on nutrition that is about as useful as the information on how to handle "cellulite." There are some excellent books and publications on the market, however, that you should read to stay abreast of this important subject. Two that I can recommend are *Jane Brody's Good Food Book: Living the High-Carbohydrate Way* and her earlier best-seller, *Nutrition.*

It is interesting to observe that our dietary link to Cro-Magnon man and woman still exists. The only foods that were available to man for hundreds of thousands of years during our evolutionary development are the foods that nutritionists are now recommending as being the most healthful. We are told to deemphasize the overfattened red meat as the focal point of each meal and place greater emphasis on vegetables, fruits, grains, and legumes (peas, beans, etc.). Those foods along with roots and nuts were essentially the daily diet of Cro-Magnon, Neanderthal, and their predecessors. Over that incredible span of time, our natural food requirements really haven't changed much. We've just gotten sidetracked.

One of the difficulties of eating smart is that too many people are eating meals prepared in corporate kitchens instead of the home kitchen. The frozen TV dinner is no longer a marital joke. With many wives working, convenience and speed become overriding considerations in meal preparation. The frozen-food section at the supermarket is bulging with every kind of entrée or enticing snack imaginable. Just pop it in the microwave, and in ten minutes you're sitting down to an effortless meal. The food never looks quite as good on your plate as the picture on the box, but it will generally satisfy your taste buds. Most important, it's fast and effortless, which seems to be the criteria we use all too often to choose our food *and* our exercise.

The corporate cooks are guided by one overriding consideration: Make sure the taste buds are happy. Consequently, they load everything with lots of salt, lots of sugar, and lots of butterfat. Some companies will promote the fact that their dishes are low in calories. But if the calories you are getting are 50 to 60 percent *fat calories*, then they are throwing you a curve.

The road to healthful eating is filled with caloric land mines. For instance, you probably are eating more chicken now than you used to because you've been told it has less cholesterol and fat. But that all depends on who's cooking it and how it's cooked. Under pressure from consumer groups, McDonald's and Burger King announced they would fry their chicken in vegetable oil. While vegetable oil is preferable to animal fat from a cholesterol standpoint, for someone fighting weight control, the real culprit is the fatty, greasy frying process itself. To lose weight and keep it off you should eliminate all fried foods and only eat things that are baked, broiled, or boiled. Good-bye, McDonald's, Burger King, and Wendy's. As a general rule you'll find that most "fast food" is fat saturated and deadly for a weight-loss program.

Most of us think we can get all the information we need on proper eating from our doctors, but that is not necessarily the case. The onrush of new nutrition information and revisions of old concepts are not getting proper emphasis in our medical schools. In November 1985, the *Tufts University Diet and Nutrition Letter* carried an article titled "Nutrition Education Lacking in Medical Schools." It reveals that a newly released National Research Council study called the quantity and quality of nutrition education most physicians receive while studying to become doctors "inadequate."

The study covered a third of the nation's medical schools and revealed that *only one in five teaches nutrition as an independent required course.* In addition, only a handful of schools emphasize the role of nutrition in promoting health and preventing disease. The article further states, "In assessing the national qualifying exam that most medical students must pass to become licensed M.D.s, the council found that less that 5 percent of the 6,000 questions screened dealt with nutrition. Even when they did, whole areas of nutrition were ignored. For example, there were no questions about diet and osteoporosis, nutritional needs of the elderly, or the relationship between diet and cancer."

If the new doctors coming out of medical schools are getting "inadequate" nutritional education, then it's reasonable to assume that many of the doctors already in practice are also ill-prepared to dispense meaningful nutritional advice. This is not meant as a criticism of the medical profession. It *is* meant to illustrate that nutrition, like exercise, is a rapidly developing subject that has taken on new importance in the last five to ten years, and we cannot assume that everybody, even our doctors, has been able to absorb it all. Doctors, in my opinion, have their hands full just keeping abreast of new medicines, new treatments, and new procedures. We have a responsibility to increase our own personal knowledge about nutrition and exercise by reading reliable publications. Three publications that I admire are *Nutrition Action* (published ten times a year by the Center for Science in the Public Interest, 1501 16th Street, NW, Washington, D.C. 20036), *Tufts University Diet and Nutrition Letter* (475 Park Avenue South, New York, NY 10016), and the University of California, Berkeley, *Wellness Letter* (available through Health Letter Associates, P.O. Box 10922, Des Moines, IA 50340).

A fine book was published in 1982 that I believe every overweight, out-of-shape person should read to clear the air once and for all about the absurdity of trying to resolve weight problems by dieting alone. The book is appropriately titled *The Dieter's Dilemma.* It was written by Dr. William Bennett, editor of the *Harvard Medical School Health Letter*, and Joel Gurin, editor of *American Health* magazine. (Both are fine publications and in a class with the ones I recommended earlier.) The book is thoroughly researched. It scientifically spells out why continuous or periodic dieting is not only futile but unhealthy.

Bennett and Gurin have a neat touch with words.

They also have a wry sense of humor, which is injected from time to time and makes what could be a boring subject enjoyable reading. In my opinion, the reason *The Dieter's Dilemma* wasn't a runaway best-seller is that it didn't deal in half-truths, fantasy, and frothy expectations. That may indicate that there are still more people who would rather have froth than fact. I hope you are not one of them. If you've reached the point in life where you really want to know the scientific truth about dieting, read *The Dieter's Dilemma.* It is published by Basic Books of New York.

The preceding recommendations for reading are an important part of your total program to whip the overweight, out-of-shape condition. The more you know about why we all are facing this dilemma, the less likely you are to get your expectations out of line with reality. Immediate dramatic results are not possible or even desirable. Pay no attention to the hype and hustle in magazines, on TV, and in fitness and diet books promising sensational results in a short time with little effort. That kind of nonsense tends to keep you off balance mentally, thinking you are doing it the hard way. You're not, however; you're doing it the right way and the only way.

The ideal approach to exercise is to start slowly and establish what your present fitness level is. Some beginners may only be able to walk a quarter of a mile at a modest pace initially. So what? You just start from there and keep pushing a little more each time out. If it takes you six months or a year to get up to an aerobic level, that's no problem. You don't win a cookie for doing it any sooner. The important thing is to keep plugging away at it. Everybody's progress will not be the same. Much will depend on the consistency and intensity you put into it. That will vary with individuals, and so will the results. If you have a slow metabolism, you will have to work harder and be more patient.

Weight loss should be slow to be effective long term. Don't try for five pounds a week. One and a half to two pounds of weight loss per week is plenty. If you are fairly heavy and do lose more rapidly the first couple of months and then the weight loss starts to taper off, don't get impatient. Your body has shifted into a slower weight-loss gear. You just keep doing all the right things and your body will follow along eventually. There is one caveat: *If you don't give the walking and the smart-eating program a minimum of three conscientious months, you will have quit too soon.* It takes about three months of constantly pushing yourself for the cumulative effects of vigorous exercise to build up. By then, the results will be so apparent, pervasive, and pleasing that the thought of going back to your former self will create a sense of panic. But that's a good panic. When you hit that level, you are hooked and on your way to becoming the trim, energetic person you want to be. You'll feel brand new.

The temptation to fall off a regular exercise program will always be present. The continuous stream of energy-saving technology has overwhelmed the overweight generation. We have lost all the legitimate reasons to expend adequate amounts of energy each day as our Cro-Magnon ancestors had to do. But the evolutionary ghosts of Cro-Magnon man and woman still control our physiological makeup. We are basically the same. The need for vigorous daily exercise is still there, and at times it almost seems the invention of the wheel was a curse instead of a blessing. Because premeditated daily aerobic exercise takes considerable discipline and determination, it is doubtful that two out of ten people will start an aerobic walking program and stay with it on the first try. I do not say that as a criticism, but as a reflection of my own struggle and the struggles of others I have observed. It was only on my third attempt over a two-year period that I could actually stick with an ongoing exercise program. And I was already over fifty years old. Quite honestly, even then it was a fluke. I was ready to quit, and if I hadn't wisecracked to Carol about men being more disciplined than women, which lit her fuse and set off a chain reaction where neither one of us *dared* to quit, I am not so sure I would have actually made it on the third try.

We are caught in the stranglehold of "the sedentary good life," and it tends to make flabby quitters out of us. Don't get discouraged if exercise doesn't come easily. If you fire and fall back, just put this book someplace where you can find it. The next time you get disgusted with yourself and say, "That's it, I've had it, I'm gonna lose this weight and get in shape," get the book out and give it another go. One of these times, you'll make it over the hump, and when you do, the only regret you'll have is that you didn't do it sooner. That's a promise.

About The Author

Casey Meyers was born in Columbus, Ohio, in 1927, and graduated with a B.A. in journalism from Ohio State University in 1950. He spent twenty-seven years in the automobile industry before retiring in 1982. Meyers owns the majority interest in two Arizona radio stations and resides in St. Joseph, Missouri.

Mr. Meyers is married and has two children. Apart from his daily aerobic walk, his favorite pastimes are quail hunting, reading, and fresh-water fishing.